A TEAM APPROACH TO
NURSING
CARE DELIVERY

Tactics for Working Better Together

ROSE O. SHERMAN

Inquiries about the book should be directed to: roseosherman@outlook.com

Author Website: www.emergingrnleader.com

ISBN: 978-1-7329127-2-4

Library of Congress Control Number: 2023903988

Published by Rose O. Sherman

Printed in the United States of America

DEDICATION

This book is dedicated to the late Dr. Eleanor C. Lambertsen, my mentor and friend, a leader in American nursing education who pioneered the concept of team nursing for better patient care.

ACKNOWLEDGMENTS

This book is about teamwork. It is important to recognize that none of us achieve our success without the support of those on our team. I have been fortunate to have great nurse mentors such as the late Marie Bastie, Dean Emeritus Anne Boykin, and Dr. Roxanne Spitzer. To Kim Martin and the team at Jera Publishing, thank you for being such pros and working with me on all three of my books.

For the content in this book, I am especially grateful to the late Dr. Eleanor Lambertsen, my friend and advisor. Dr. Lambertsen pioneered and studied the concept of team-based nursing care at the end of World War II with a Kellogg Foundation Grant. Thirty years ago, toward the end of her life, she mentored me at Teachers College, Columbia University, as I did my dissertation research on the team-based approach to care used in the Department of Veterans Affairs. Team nursing had fallen into disfavor at that time as most systems adopted a primary nursing care model. I asked Eleanor how she felt, and I will never forget her prediction that a team approach to care delivery would return, maybe not in her lifetime, but it would. I am sure she was up there smiling as I wrote this book.

During the last three years, along with my technology facilitator Jim Frey, we have done hundreds of virtual nursing leadership workshops attended by thousands of nurse leaders. They have shared their stories with us, and I have included many of them in this book. I am grateful for their honesty and insights. It is hard to be a nurse leader in the current environment, and I am so thankful for those of you serving in these roles today.

To my family – my husband Jim, always my biggest supporter; my son Mark; his wife Jenn; and our grandchildren John and Beverly Rose, you always inspire me to do better work.

FOREWORD

It may only come around once in a lifetime. You meet one person that alters the course of your professional career. Then you realize, she is not just your personal spark, but a flame for the entire nursing profession. Dr. Rose Sherman EdD, RN, NEA-BC, FAAN is this catalyst. She is there to serve the profession, the professional, and ultimately the patient. She is a mentor's mentor, sharing her time, talent, and treasures with thousands of nurse leaders throughout the years.

This book, A Team Approach to Nursing Care Delivery, is her third. She once again imparts wisdom, garnered over the course of a stellar career. She comes by this wisdom the hard way, researching, interviewing, writing, editing, and speaking. It is through the facilitation of discourse throughout the country, that she comes to know and understand the condition of the American nurse and the state of the practice environment. The question remains, however, are you ready to listen?

There is a concept in nursing education called, "readiness to learn." Practicing nurses may encounter what they consider to be apathetic patients; unwilling to listen to evidence-based advice related to their varying conditions. They may not be apathetic. They might just not be ready to learn. Perhaps they are in pain, in denial, or preoccupied with life's challenges. Despite well-scripted tools, they remain "non-compliant," not yet ready to seek wellness. However, maybe tomorrow, the week after, or at the next admission, their situation is different, and they seek out information.

It's like this with nursing leaders. How quick are they to say, "Oh, we tried that already, and it did not work!" "Team nursing, oh yeah well, LPNs cannot do assessments, so why bother having them. It's extra work for the RNS, or RNs can just as easily bathe patients, as the CNAs. Besides, they can assess the skin while they are doing that!" There is so much written in the literature regarding the concept, of RN "top of practice." This describes an environment where RNs assess, plan, implement, and evaluate the individualized care of a patient. Other care partners round out the team and participate to the fullest extent of their own licenses.

The tumultuous nature of health care, impeded by a worldwide pandemic, and fueled by ever-changing societal issues, has created unprecedented challenges. However, along with these challenges is the realization that wisdom, tools, and innovations exist to help find solutions. It is absolutely critical to collaborate to build on solid ideas, revitalizing them to solve problems. Can there be a better argument for the resurgence of team care delivery?

Once again, Dr. Rose Sherman is the catalyst, sparking the profession to rethink a team approach to nursing care delivery. She wants nurse leaders to imagine, the positive impact multiple specialties working in unison, at the top of their practice, can have on both the patient and the caregivers. Now is the time. Are you ready to learn?

Angela S. Prestia Ph.D. RN NE-BC   April 2023

INTRODUCTION

Leadership author John Maxwell cited the Law of Everest in his work on teamwork. As challenges in the environment escalate, he observes, the need for teamwork elevates. Few nurse leaders would disagree with this assessment as we try to navigate the turbulence and turmoil in healthcare in our post-pandemic environment.

There is power in teamwork, and teams will generally outperform individuals. When you bring together healthcare staff with complementary skills, a shared purpose, and mutual accountability, a synergy develops that can overcome the greatest challenges. But in a crisis, even the most effective teams can unravel. We watched this happen during COVID as individual team members were overwhelmed by this life-quake experience, leading them to question how they should move forward in their personal lives and careers.

As I write this book, we have one of the most severe labor shortages ever experienced in nursing and healthcare. Staff turnover and vacancy rates have skyrocketed even in the best health systems. The current healthcare delivery models rely on the availability of many nurses and are unsustainable. The gap between the number of nurses needed to practice primary nursing and the number of nurses available cannot be effectively bridged even with a significant ramp-up in enrollments and certainly not in a cost-effective way.

Outside of a few specialty areas, future care delivery models will necessitate a team-based approach with professionals and support staff all working at the top of their scope of practice. While we once had the luxury of assigning nurses to non-nursing tasks, the situation has changed, and we no longer can. Yet, the transition to a team or collaborative care model is challenging despite the need. Most young nurses today lack the leadership skills to delegate care and manage a team of care providers. It will also require a change in mindset among nurses from thinking about "my patients" to thinking about "our patients" as nurses co-manage more patients.

This book, *A Team Approach to Nursing Care Delivery: Tactics for Working Better Together,* provides a roadmap of what to consider as you redesign care and rebuild teams. Whether you are in your first year of leadership or have decades of experience, nurse leaders now face unprecedented challenges as they work to redesign care delivery systems. A leader recently noted in a leadership session that although we know we need to do this, it will be a very tough sell to many of our nurses who have never practiced a team-based approach to care. It is like building a plane at the same time you are flying it with a full load of passengers.

In an easy-to-read format, each chapter in this book includes stories of challenges and successes that leaders have shared with me about team-based care delivery and efforts to promote effective teamwork. I aim to help you learn from their experiences and insights and acquire new evidence-based leadership strategies and tactics. Let this book be your toolkit and practical guide to fostering effective team-based care delivery regardless of your clinical setting.

CONTENTS

PART 1

REDESIGNING NURSING CARE DELIVERY

"You cannot swim for new horizons unless you have the courage to lose sight of the shore."

WILLIAM FAULKNER

CHAPTER 1

UNDERSTANDING THE
FORCES FOR CHANGE

Sherry has been a critical care director for ten years and a nurse for more than two decades. She divides her career into two parts. The first part was the years before COVID, and while there were staffing challenges and nursing shortages, it was nothing like today. The second part of her career is in the post-COVID environment. She now spends about 70% of her time on staffing and scheduling. Most of her staff are young nurses with limited critical care experience. Patient acuity is high, and her census rarely drops below 90%. Her health system is struggling with financial problems and has challenges keeping pace with the cost of labor and supplies. The turnover on Sherry's team is high, and staff is battling exhaustion and burnout. She doubts whether the current trajectory of her unit is sustainable but is unsure what changes could help stabilize her team.

Most nurse leaders can relate to Sherry's story. The COVID-19 experience has massively disrupted most health systems and the lives of staff members. Life transitions such as births, deaths, marriages, or new jobs can significantly impact our roles, responsibilities, assumptions, and routines. Some life events fall into a different category and are called life-quakes. COVID-19 is an excellent example of a life event that became a global life quake. In his book *Life is in the Transitions*, Bruce Feiler describes a life-quake as a massive life change high on the Richter scale of consequences that has aftershocks for years.[1] When people experience life-quakes, their top two emotions are fear and sadness.

Nurse leaders have seen these emotions in their staff as they face the reality that the future will not be like the past. The good news is that life-quakes do not last forever. We transition through three phases as we move through life-quake events (Figure 1). The first phase is the long goodbye. In this phase, you realize that you must let go of some aspects of the past. Sometimes, we can get stuck in grief over what we have lost and have difficulty moving forward. The second phase is the messy middle. This messy middle can last for an extended time and is complex. During this phase, we shed habits, routines, and beliefs that no longer work for us. During this messy middle, we can be at our creative best because we need to be to heal. The final phase is a new beginning when we grow comfortable with our new lives. Life-quakes are an important reminder that none of us lead linear lives with predictable outcomes. Transitions will always be part of life and require us to make changes.

Moving to a new beginning is challenging because it forces us to revisit some of our long-held values and beliefs that are sometimes hard to release. Professional writers know how hard it can be to "kill your darlings." In writing, you kill your darlings when you eliminate an unnecessary storyline, character, or sentence - elements you may have worked hard to create but must remove for the sake of your overall story. It is a good metaphor for redesigning nursing care delivery models in health systems today. For decades, most acute care nursing settings have used primary nursing. Nurses worked twelve-hour schedules almost exclusively. These approaches to care delivery worked in the past but no longer. Nurses want greater flexibility in their work and shorter tours of duty. The gap between the number of nurses needed and the availability of nursing candidates has widened, making primary nursing care delivery difficult.

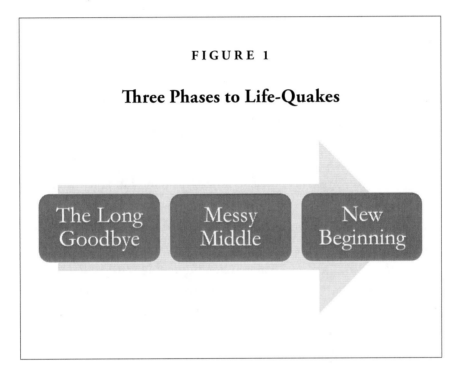

FIGURE 1

Three Phases to Life-Quakes

The Long Goodbye — Messy Middle — New Beginning

THE GREAT NURSING RESET

Like Sherry, Marcus has seen significant changes in the perioperative workforce he manages. Before COVID, his staff were experienced in their specialty area, and turnover was low. During COVID, elective surgeries were canceled, and OR nurses were either redeployed to other areas or furloughed. This disruption caused team anger and negativity.

Many of his staff retired early, and some indicated that they planned to leave the profession. Others have converted to part-time schedules. He could not fill his vacancies with experienced OR nurses for the first time in his leadership tenure. Even surgical technicians are now in short supply. At great expense to his organization, Marcus uses travel nurses as part of his core staffing. He now hires and orients new graduates to the OR but finds they rarely stay more than a couple of years. His team seems less connected to one another. The sense of community on the team is lacking.

Leaders like Sherry and Marcus have seen the great nursing reset on their teams. Nurses view their careers differently as an outcome of the COVID life-quake experience. Nurses now consider mental health and well-being as high priorities in work-life decisions. There is a reluctance to work weekends, nights, or additional shifts. The newest generation of nurses, Generation Z (born 1997-2012), sees jobs as *tours of duty* in a more extensive career trajectory, so long-term retention at the unit level is probably unrealistic.[2] The implications of these changes from strong core teams where staff work together for long periods to a teaming environment where tenures are shorter are discussed in Chapter 4.

COVID also accelerated massive demographic shifts in the nursing profession that would have naturally occurred. In a comprehensive 2020 workforce report, the National Council of State Boards of Nursing sounded the alarm bells with the following statistics:[3]

- The average age of a nurse in the US in 2020 was 52.
- 19% of the RN workforce were over 65; while licensed, many were not working.
- 54% of nurses worked in hospital settings – a steady decline over the past three decades.
- 65.2% of nurses have BSNs, giving them more employment options.
- 20% of nurses surveyed planned to retire within five years.
- Only 64.9% of nurses worked full-time.

Nursing workforce forecasters now estimate a nursing shortage of up to one million nurses by 2030.[4] The deficits are already being felt, with a national vacancy rate that exceeds 17%.[5] Despite national discussion about a moonshot type of initiative to promote the expansion of nursing graduates, nursing education programs currently have significant faculty shortages. Building a pipeline in time to meet the growing need for nurses is probably impossible. The hardest hit employers in the competition for nurses will be acute and long-term care settings. Improving work environments and offering better work-life balance will improve retention but will not be enough to meet future staffing needs.

Maria has seen the impact of staffing shortages in her medical-surgical unit. She tracked workforce data and was not surprised to see an ANA Pulse survey indicating that 55% of nurses reported their units had the appropriate number of RNs less than half the time.[6] The issues reported in this survey are ones Maria experiences in her unit. She has problems scheduling staff for vacation during the timeframes requested and frequently asks staff to work additional shifts. Maintaining staff morale with staffing shortages has been challenging. Even new graduates that Maria might have successfully hired in the past for her unit now have so many employment opportunities that they can quickly move right into subspecialty areas like critical care or labor and delivery.

Although Maria has maintained a pulse on what is happening in nursing, many of her staff have not. When she reviews workforce research with her team, they seem surprised at how pervasive the shortages are, and some argue that mandated staffing ratios are the solution to the problem. Maria understands that the sustainability of her unit will be contingent on redesigning care from primary nursing to a more team-based approach. Still, she worries that nurses will resist the necessary innovations. The nursing mindset must shift from thinking about "my patients" to "our patients" as nurses manage larger assignments. She also worries that young nurses today lack the leadership skills needed to delegate care and manage a team of care providers

CHANGES IN HEALTHCARE DEMAND
AND REIMBURSEMENT

Forces beyond nurse staffing also drive a need for a change in care delivery. The demand for patient care is increasing. The percentage of 60-90-year-olds in the US population is expected to grow significantly in the next decade. By 2030 more than 20% of the US population will be over 65.[7] This segment of the population has the highest utilization of health services. We already see these trends in health systems today. Hospital volumes have increased, and the pressure for services will only build. At this same time, health systems struggle to keep pace with rising labor costs and virtually everything else. Neither consumers nor insurance payers will accept steep increases in prices.

Healthcare costs in the United States are already the highest globally, yet patient outcomes are often not as good. Our traditional payment methodology contributes to healthcare's overall cost in this country. Under the historical fee-for-service reimbursement model, the incentive is to provide more care. Payment incentives are moving away from this volume-oriented approach toward a greater focus on the value of services and health outcomes, including fewer hospitalizations. Consumers also want more price transparency at the point of service. Hospitals and providers will assume more risk and must ensure that the services are low-cost and high-quality. The many performance measures tracked in every area of patient care, such as hospital readmissions, patient falls, and patient satisfaction, will continue to have a significant impact on reimbursement in a value-focused environment

Value-based programs reward healthcare providers with incentive payments for the quality of care to those covered under Medicare. These programs are part of a broader quality strategy to reform how health care is delivered and reimbursed. Health systems receive higher payments when they can avoid costs associated with problems like patient falls, infections, or readmissions. As an outcome of the impact of COVID on health systems and the turnover of healthcare teams, the Institute for Healthcare Improvement (IHI), the Centers for Medicare and Medicaid (CMS), and the Joint Commission have all sounded alarm bells about a decline in quality performance metrics.[8]

In many respects, the move to value-based purchasing presents a strong argument for more team-based care. In the fee-for-service system, service payments were negotiated and paid for in silos, even within the same health system. Historically, patients admitted for a specific procedure, such as a total hip replacement, were billed separately for laboratory, rehabilitation, physician services, and hospitalization. With this level of fragmentation, there was no financial incentive for healthcare teams to work together to create value. Bundled payments that are now part of value-based systems have changed the incentives to promote stronger teamwork and care coordination.

Changing payment models, regulatory requirements, cost containment pressures, and disruptive competition are among the challenges facing leaders in today's healthcare environment. Jake is learning this in his new cardiac procedural unit director role. For years, his area was a profit center for his organization. Several large employers in his area now want a bundled price for cardiac interventional procedures. Considerable increases in the cost of supplies and the ongoing use of travel nurses to supplement his staffing have negatively impacted the unit's budget and the cost of care. Jake tries to do as much or more with decreasing resources but finds his current staffing model challenging. Maintaining quality and safety metrics is essential to Jake's organization's bottom line and will help determine whether they are awarded bundled care contracts. He now reviews ways to change care delivery to lower costs and improve quality.

IMPLICATIONS FOR NURSING CARE DELIVERY

The American Association of Critical Care Nursing convened a staffing think-tank in 2022. Their final report noted that while the work of nurses has changed dramatically, models for care delivery remain static.

The think tank members prioritized innovation in care delivery models, which includes changing our approach to in-person/onsite care, expanding virtual care delivery, and leveraging remote monitoring technology. The recommendations emphasize having nurses in all stages of planning and implementing innovative models for care delivery.[9] Most nurse leaders realize that delivering primary nursing care in all specialty areas will be impossible, given the forces of change discussed in this chapter. Staffing plans that assign nurses to care for 8-10 acutely ill patients and describe it as primary nursing are incompatible with that delivery model.

Different approaches to nursing care delivery have evolved over the past five decades. Most hospitals used a team approach to care from World War II through the early 1980s. Beginning in the 1980s, primary nursing care models replaced team nursing. In the primary nursing model, RNs accept responsibility for administering and coordinating all aspects of the patient's nursing care. LPNs are rarely employed in acute care environments using this care delivery model. Primary nursing care aims to promote continuity of care across the length of stay, with nurses having greater insight into the patient's medical and emotional condition. For effective primary care delivery, nurse-patient ratios need to be relatively low. The shortage of nurses, the implementation of 12-hour tours, the addition of travel nurses, and a move to shorter patient lengths of stay have led to challenges in promoting the continuity of care that were the cornerstone of the primary nursing care model.

Over the last four decades, primary nurses have taken on many responsibilities that other team members could do. On a webinar, Melinda Stibal, a CNO in the Legacy health system, shared that their research indicates 48% of what nurses do today doesn't require a nursing license.[10] She noted the only way to move forward is to optimize the role of the RN. Albert Einstein wisely reminded us, *"You cannot solve a problem with the same thinking that created the problem."*[11] Today's challenges demand a different approach to how we think about care delivery. Healthcare leaders are now beginning to understand the need for change. In a recent *Models of Care Insight Study,*

66% of leaders surveyed see a need for improvement, and 70% now consider changing their models.[12] Future nursing care delivery models must involve other team members who work together to provide care.

A TEAM-BASED APPROACH TO CARE DELIVERY

Team-based care models provide health services to individuals, families, and communities using at least two health providers who work collaboratively with patients and their caregivers to accomplish shared goals within and across care settings to achieve coordinated, high-quality care.[13] The care team can include many different types of healthcare professionals and non-professionals depending on the specialty setting and needs of the patients. Historically, nursing teams have included RN, LPN, CNA, or PCT roles. Team-based care was used widely throughout the COVID crisis during patient surges when even non-clinical staff were redeployed into critical care areas or COVID units to assist in giving care.

Today, creative organizations now look at adding other positions to the direct care team, including EMTs, pharmacists, therapists, exercise physiologists, ARNPs, CNLs, CNSs, student nurses, and other care team associates. Some team members may work virtually, providing surveillance, patient education, consultation backup, and doing time-consuming tasks such as admissions and discharges. We also see robots like Moxie as part of the care team, assisting with non-clinical activities such as delivering medication and supplies. With technological advancements, robots will soon move into more clinically focused activities, including patient surveillance and assessment activities.[14]

An example of a new contemporary team-based model described above is one that Trinity Health Michigan is piloting. The Virtual Connected Care Program provides a three-person care team model that works in tandem to provide for the patient's needs.[15] The health care delivery model involves three people: the direct care nurse, the virtual nurse, and the licensed practical nurse. The model is designed with an on-unit RN directing care. With the patient's permission, the virtual nurse can enter an encounter with the patient. They ensure that the patient understands the care plan for the day and provide backup support for the on-unit RN and LPN.

In the Trinity model, the patient does not have to press a call bell and wait for a response. The patient can initiate the encounter with the virtual nurse, and the answer is almost immediate. Virtual nurses are integral in coordinating care and communication with the interdisciplinary team and are involved in discharge planning rounds. They can arrange for discharge teaching and ensure that the patient understands everything communicated to them. Another benefit is the ability of the virtual model to pair early career nurses at the bedside with more experienced virtual nurses who can provide critical thinking and expertise to help younger nurses as needed. Seasoned nurses can stay in the workforce longer without the physical demands of doing direct patient care. The ultimate plan at Trinity is to roll this new model out system-wide. A similar approach to care is now evolving in the Atrium Health System. Virtual nurses are assigned to ten patients to support novice RNs on the unit. They do admission assessments, charting, medication reconciliation, and physician rounding. Early outcomes are promising and include reduced patient falls, improved patient experiences, and increased nurse satisfaction.[16]

Team-based care has also been introduced at Texas Memorial Hermann with good outcomes. A Kaizen was held with the frontline team, breaking down all care tasks required for care into licensed and skill-specific tasks. It was identified that 40% of the work currently performed by RNs could be safely delegated to other team members. A team approach model that utilized licensed vocational nurses, doulas, and ancillary support was piloted for six months, including clinical-based orientation and a charge nurse development guide on roles and responsibilities. The new model impacted efficiency and patient and quality outcomes across the service line. After the pilot was completed, the length of stay observed/expected was within the top quartile of a national peer database, decreased severe maternal morbidity cases (complications associated with delivery) went from 2.8% to 0.0% from January 2022 to July 2022, annualized turnover of 32.4% improved to 19.4% in six months (3.5% in August 2022) and employee engagement scores advanced after the pilot.[17]

TEAM NURSING REVISITED.

The concept of a team or collaborative approach to care is not new. Team nursing care initially developed during a nursing workforce crisis in World War II. With registered nurses in short supply, the military trained ancillary healthcare staff, including medical corpsmen and 91 Charlies (with LPN responsibilities), to work with nurses using a team approach to care. After the war, the VA Health System employed these military-trained ancillary healthcare staff and adopted the team nursing model. Most VA Medical Centers continue to use team-based care as their delivery model.

The team nursing delivery system was studied in the late 1940s and early 1950s by Dr. Eleanor Lambertsen at Teachers College Columbia University with a Kellogg Foundation grant. Her research found the team approach to care was efficient and effective in producing good patient outcomes. Dr. Lambertson's work attracted nursing administrators nationwide who sought to reorganize their nursing staff. A guiding principle of team nursing is that multiple healthcare professionals working together can provide a higher level of care than any single professional working alone. In the team nursing model, each team member has specific responsibilities and works together to provide comprehensive patient care. Teams are led by nurses who assume responsibility for overall care coordination.[18]

An unexpected outcome of the model was that it did promote the idea of career mobility in nursing. Many team members went back to school with the help of their organizations to become RNs. In interviews that I conducted with Dr. Lambertsen in the 1990s, she noted team nursing requires nurses to take leadership in patient care and fully utilize the skills and abilities of all their team members. Not every nurse she observed was ready, willing, or able to do this, especially when most at the time were not baccalaureate-prepared. Few organizations took the time to teach the leadership and teamwork skills needed to implement the model effectively.[19] Another challenge was the misconception that professional nurses don't deliver direct care in a team nursing model.

Part of the resistance today to a team-based care approach is that some nurse leaders have bad memories of their experiences with team nursing in settings where it was poorly executed. Younger nurses and many newer leaders know little about it and don't want to revisit the past. Yet with careful planning and strong execution, a team-based care delivery model can be successful. Changing a delivery model may mean sacrificing some sacred cows. The current healthcare environment challenges the sense of order for many nurses with long professional careers. When we feel fearful, it can be comforting to cling to what we know has worked in the past, but unfortunately, we can't do this moving into the future if our goal is to improve care.

Key Points

✓ The COVID-19 experience has changed how nurses view their lives and their work.

✓ The current nursing shortage is unprecedented and could lead to one million nursing vacancies.

✓ There is a critical need to redesign the delivery of nursing care.

✓ A team-based care model of nursing delivery is an approach that offers opportunities to improve care and reduce costs.

✓ Changing a delivery model may mean sacrificing some sacred cows.

CHAPTER 2

PLANNING FOR A TEAM APPROACH TO CARE DELIVERY

N ate is the new CNO in a hospital struggling to recruit and retain staff. While the staffing plan is one RN for five patients on their medical-surgical units, this goal is rarely achieved. As Nate considers the nursing workforce challenges in his geographic area, he recognizes that their current staffing strategies are unrealistic and a new approach to care delivery is needed. During his interview for the CNO role, he was asked about his ideas for innovation. Nate pointed out that one of the challenges in redesigning care delivery is that each specialty area and outpatient clinic have different needs. Given his experience, he thought a new model should include a team-based care delivery framework emphasizing patient-centered care. He carefully explained that, as an organization, they would never have control over the supply of RNs, but they did have control over how they used their resources to deliver care.

Nate shared with the interview committee that he had seen team-based care work well during his time in the military. Every officer and enlisted team member worked to the top of their rank and scope of practice. A team-based framework would allow for flexibility in team composition driven by patient needs and staff availability. He envisioned the teams as nurse-led but conceded that it would take time to develop the staff to do this. When he left military service and entered the civilian healthcare world, he was shocked at the lack of teamwork. Every nurse seemed to be siloed into caring for their patients, and team backup was noticeably absent.

Nate is wise enough to realize that any change in delivering care requires careful planning. He does not have the luxury of closing units to redesign care delivery. He had read *The Seven Habits of Highly Effective People* by Stephen Covey early in his career. [20] One of the habits is to begin with the end in mind. This habit promotes proactive planning and recommends that you identify in advance what goals you want to achieve. Carpenters understand the importance of measuring twice, so you only cut once. Yet too often, we fail to do this, and projects don't achieve the anticipated results. Covey talks about leaders being so busy cutting the undergrowth that they fail to realize they are in the wrong jungle.

As Nate works with his team to redesign care, he will want to use human-centered design principles (HCD), which puts the person first by capturing the end user's thoughts, feelings, experiences, and challenges. In redesigning care delivery, you have two end users: the team delivering care and the patient receiving it. You want to *frame the change* to prioritize the end users to ensure relevant and effective solutions and avoid assumptions that might not be valid. You want to *be intentional* in solving the problem correctly, respecting end users' lived experiences, needs, and priorities. Finally, you want to *ensure that there is a collaboration* with end users in the redesigning process to create a new care design and test ideas. [21]

With human-centered design as a framework, Nate could then use the four-step process to redesign care recommended by the Agency for Healthcare Research and Quality ((Figure 2).[22]

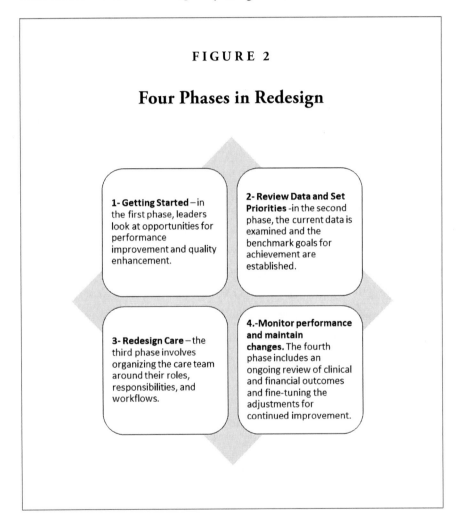

FIGURE 2

Four Phases in Redesign

1- Getting Started – in the first phase, leaders look at opportunities for performance improvement and quality enhancement.

2- Review Data and Set Priorities - in the second phase, the current data is examined and the benchmark goals for achievement are established.

3- Redesign Care – the third phase involves organizing the care team around their roles, responsibilities, and workflows.

4.-Monitor performance and maintain changes. The fourth phase includes an ongoing review of clinical and financial outcomes and fine-tuning the adjustments for continued improvement.

PHASE 1 - GETTING STARTED

To start the planning, Nate brings together his leadership team for a strategic planning session to discuss redesigning care delivery. Nate believes every problem is an idea problem and that the best ideas will come from his very talented frontline leaders. His goal is to generate as many ideas as possible. Research indicates that creative problem-solving and innovation are most effective when done collaboratively.

Nate presents the nurse leaders with the following ten questions for discussion:

1. What would we do if we were planning a new hospital and had the opportunity to design an entirely different care delivery?'
2. What are the most time-consuming activities for RNs that others could do?
3. What workflow and geographic space challenges consume RN time?
4. What equipment challenges do we have that impact care delivery?
5. What parts of our nursing care could we eliminate or reduce and lose very little value for the patient?
6. Can we look beyond traditional healthcare team members to support inpatient care using other team members?
7. What is the availability of support staff in our community?
8. If we move to a team-based approach to care, what needs to happen to change the current RN mindset and upskill our RN workforce in teamwork, supervision, and delegation skills?
9. Which of our units within the hospital might be a good fit for a pilot project?
10. Who should be on the care delivery redesign team, so we don't overlook critical stakeholders?

Nate was pleasantly surprised with the engagement level and great ideas from the planning session. He learned that medication administration, admission and discharge documentation, and hunting for supplies consumed large amounts of RN time. The leaders felt that any care redesign needed to include strategies to offload parts of these activities. He also discovered that who needed to be on teams varied widely across specialties. The nursing leaders pointed out to Nate that most of the redesign changes proposed would lead to nurses assuming more responsibility for care coordination and team management. These changes in the RN role might meet resistance and require staff education and ongoing coaching. They also worried about the lack of teamwork they observed on their teams and mentioned how crucial rebuilding this teamwork would be to care redesign.

PHASE 2 - REVIEW DATA AND SET PRIORITIES

While leaders like Nate may want to implement a delivery model change across their whole organization simultaneously, a more thoughtful approach is to select one area to begin the innovation and test your assumptions. In addition to the retreat feedback he received, Nate will also want to look at data before setting the benchmark goals. Some key data points to review could include staff demographics, recruitment and retention data, nurse satisfaction data, patient satisfaction scores, length of stay, the staffing budget, the use of agency or travel nurses, and the current skill mix of staff. Nate might also want to use a team-work assessment tool (Chapter 4 Toolkit) to obtain baseline data before implementing the model. Another survey that could be added measures missed nursing care before and after implementation.[23] Nate's team may decide to include NDNQI performance indicators to evaluate the changes in the skill mix. The following indicators are essential benchmarks to assess the impact of the new team-based model:

- Nurse hours per patient day
- Nursing turnover
- Nosocomial infections
- Patient falls and falls with injury

- Development of pressure ulcers
- Restraint usage
- Nurse practice environment

Reviewing this data will help to pinpoint areas needed for improvement and ultimately help evaluate the outcomes of a new care delivery model.

PHASE 3 - REDESIGN CARE

The next essential step is to redesign care. Revamping care delivery is a complex step because the scope and responsibilities in each role must be defined, and the unit's workflow should be assessed. Patient care units can be considered clinical microsystems. Each unit has small, interdependent groups working together regularly to care for specific patients. The Institute for Healthcare Improvement provides free assessment tools designed by quality experts at Dartmouth Hitchcock to evaluate current unit processes and microsystem functioning.[24]

Some key unit processes to assess include:

- Leadership structure
- Assignment of admissions
- Current hours per patient day of care
- Discharge planning
- Communication with physicians
- Management of new patient orders
- Shift reports and huddles
- Frequency of patient rounding
- Documentation requirements
- Patient handoffs to other areas
- The process of obtaining supplies and equipment
- Patient transport

- Medication administration
- Unit onboarding
- Communication mechanisms with other staff members
- Sitter protocols
- Skin assessment

In changing to a team-based care approach, an initial step is to look at the current roles used in the specialty to determine who assumes accountability for the critical processes discussed above. Review organizational position descriptions and policies but recognize that they may not reflect all the role responsibilities of current staff. For some functions, you may need to flowchart current practices.

Evaluate your state's legal scope of practice for each role you may add to the team. Although there are similarities across state practice acts and statutes, some states have broader practice acts than others. Reviewing this information must be the first step before designing job descriptions and organizational policies. Ideally, the goal should be to have each team member working to the top of their scope of practice. It is at this step that you should also identify educational development needs. Just because a responsibility might be part of a scope of practice does not mean the staff member has the necessary competency. Learning needs should be identified and training provided before the new responsibilities are assumed. You may, as an example, decide to expand the role of the patient care technician to include enhanced tasks such as simple dressing changes, oxygen set-up, performing glucose testing, or discontinuing foley catheters. If you add LPNs to the team, some states will allow them to administer intravenous medications and start intravenous lines.

Adding team members will require changes in position descriptions and processes, such as a change in shift reports and patient rounding. In a team-based approach to care, there needs to be a nurse team leader designated who is responsible for coordinating care for a group of patients. A leader is vital to success in a team-based model of care. They need to have both leadership abilities and strong clinical skills. They must determine how to delegate and distribute the workload while aligning core staff competencies with patient and family needs. New team leaders may worry about the new responsibilities' impact on their professional liability and license. Nurses selected to be team leaders need enhanced training in supervision, delegation, and other team-leading skills discussed in future chapters of this book. Providing clarity in role function is essential.

Throughout the planning process, it is crucial to include key stakeholders who may not be part of the new team but could be impacted by changes in how care is delivered or different unit processes. This part of the redesign process is sometimes overlooked and can result in unintended consequences that influence successful implementation. Using the RACI Model for decision-making can help with this.

The RACI Model for Decision-Making

Responsible – who owns the decision or problem.

Accountable – who is responsible or accountable for seeing the decision is made and implemented.

Consulted – who needs to be consulted in addressing the problem or making the decision.

Informed – who should be informed about the decision or problem resolution.

Dietary, imaging, lab, and environmental services departments should have an opportunity to review the new car delivery plan. Involve human resource partners in discussions about new roles on the team.

Engage your physician colleagues as they will interface with team members when rounding on units. It is also essential to speak with your academic partners about your redesign efforts, as a change in care delivery may impact the competencies new graduates need to work effectively in the model. In unionized workplaces, it is vital to keep union partners informed of any changes in practices that could change work conditions.

Phase 4 - Monitor Performance and Maintain Changes

The last phase in implementing a new care delivery model is the execution of the plan and ongoing review. As with any new initiative, not everything will work or go as planned. Modifications will be needed. The Plan-Do-Study-Act (PDSA) method is a way to test a change during implementation.[25] Going through the prescribed four steps guides the thinking process into breaking down the task into steps and then evaluating the outcomes, improving on them, and testing again. Having the new methods written down and reviewed regularly will help team members focus on what is working and what may need to be changed.

At this stage, it is essential to measure whether the goals established in Step 2 are being met. You will also want to explore any unintended consequences of a change in care delivery, both good and bad. Team-based care is impossible without solid nursing leadership and clear communication. Leadership skill in these areas requires ongoing evaluation. In a team-based model, team members share accountability for patient care. Ensuring that things don't fall between the cracks requires continuous monitoring. We will discuss specific strategies to promote team accountability in Chapter 10.

Managing Resistance to Change

Today's healthcare environment is volatile, uncertain, complex, and ambiguous. At no time was that more apparent than during the recent COVID pandemic. The pace of change has been challenging for healthcare staff, and many leaders are dealing with negativity and resistance to change. Resistance to change should not be surprising if you plan to deliver care differently. When a change in care delivery happens, staff need to learn new behaviors, and old ones must be unlearned.

Changes in care delivery are complicated because our practices are, in essence, a collection of habits. Charles Duhigg, an investigative reporter for the New York Times, wrote an interesting evidence-based book about how habits form and how we can change them.[26] Duhigg contends that habits make up 40% of our daily routines, whether at work or home. What you see in your work environments are habits that develop over time. Habits are the brain's way of saving energy. They allow us to work on autopilot. A mistake that leaders make is that they forget how ingrained habits are. Hardwiring a new habit can take more than the 30 days we often devote to implementing new initiatives. That's why change can be so challenging. It is also why experienced staff may have more challenges with change than novices. Practice habits become hardwired over time. Any new habit or practice change may feel threatening. Asking a nurse with only primary care experience to be a team leader is a shift in role expectations. Significant change can make staff feel psychologically unsafe because the brain perceives it as a threat.

You have probably noticed that not all staff accept change in the same way or on the same timeline. In his work on the diffusion of innovation, Everett Rogers discovered that acceptance of innovation or change is on a bell curve (Figure 3).[27]

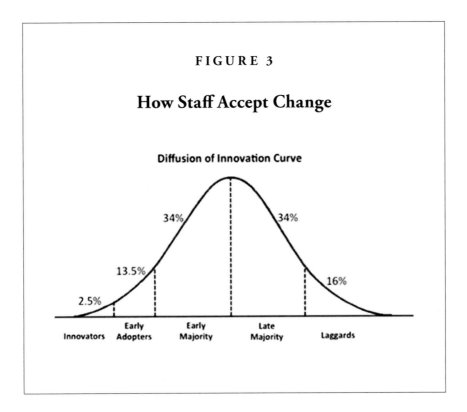

FIGURE 3

How Staff Accept Change

Diffusion of Innovation Curve

34%   34%

13.5%

16%

2.5%

| Innovators | Early Adopters | Early Majority | Late Majority | Laggards |

Some nurses are natural innovators or early adopters. Other staff will be slow to adopt change. Nurse leaders need to meet team members where they are in the change process. Changing parts of one's practice can be emotional. It often means letting go of something you have valued in the past. During times of rapid change, staff can feel psychologically unsafe. Your team depends on you to help them understand the meaning of the change – why it is needed and how it will impact them. The language leaders use to frame change significantly affects how individuals make sense of the world and their actions.

You will observe distinct behavioral patterns in how staff respond to change. Kerry Bunker identifies four ways staff responds to change (e.g. *Entrenched, Overwhelmed, Poser, or Learner*). [28] Entrenched staff may decide that they can outlast change – ex. Maybe it will not happen until I retire. Overwhelmed staff have high anxiety levels during a change and may have feelings of depression or powerlessness. Posers exhibit high confidence in dealing with changes but may not have the necessary self-awareness and competence. Learners feel challenged and stretched but are determined to move forward. They seek learning opportunities to expand their skills in response to the change. Learners can be a leader's best ally in helping other staff transition during changes.

Driving change can be incredibly challenging with entrenched staff. Karen's medical-surgical unit participated as a pilot unit for a team-based care delivery model. She experienced significant negativity and resistance from some staff who called the initiative the "flavor of the month." She had several nurses she described as CAVE dwellers or staff who are **C**onsistently – **A**gainst – **V**irtually – **E**verything. Despite the urgency of changing the care delivery model, Karen struggled to get them on board. Chapter 9 will discuss strategies for working with difficult team members.

Once you commit to changing a care delivery model, you can give the team time to vent but not to debate the decision. The planned timeline for the change is non-negotiable. Once you have done that, shift the discussion to the future. Leaders who remain calm, truthful, and optimistic in their communications help prevent misinformation and reduce staff anxiety. There are silver linings in almost any situation, and the leader needs to be the first to help everyone see what they are. An optimistic attitude and outlook on the part of the leader can be energizing and contagious. It will motivate your staff to do their best. You need to expect success if you are to achieve it.

Key Points

✓ There are four phases to redesigning care delivery.

✓ Establish the priorities and set outcome goals before implementing a care delivery redesign.

✓ The Plan-Do-Study-Act (PDSA) method is a way to test a change and make needed modifications.

✓ Expect resistance to change if you plan to deliver care differently.

✓ Leaders who remain calm, truthful, and optimistic in their communications help prevent misinformation and reduce staff anxiety.

CHAPTER 3

RESETTING THE ROLE OF MANAGER

Steve has been an oncology unit manager for six years. In the pre-COVID environment, his team was stable. He had little trouble recruiting and retaining oncology-certified nurses. Fast forward to today, and he finds himself in a different environment with his team. Over the past two years, many of his experienced nurses have retired. His core team now does not have the depth or breadth of experience they once had. When he interviews new graduates, they have career plans that don't include spending more than one or two years on his unit. When Steve compares managing today to when he first began, he sees changes in his role and what it requires of him. Some of the differences he notes include the following:

- His span of control is much broader as many of his staff now work part-time.
- He provides more hands-on coaching and mentoring of new staff as he has fewer experienced preceptors on his team.

- He now spends 60-80% of his time on recruitment, scheduling, and staffing.
- Work-life balance seems harder to achieve.
- He has seen a shift in staff attitudes about teamwork and a move toward transactional relationships focusing on cash compensation.
- His staff's mental health and well-being are now priority concerns for him.
- Patients and families complain more and show less respect for the staff.
- Support services his staff depends on also have staffing challenges.

Steve's experience in his frontline leadership role is not unusual. The American Organization of Nurse Leaders (AONL) convened a subgroup to examine nurse manager recruitment and retention. Their data indicates that 45% of frontline leaders are considering leaving their positions.[29] The turmoil, turbulence, and turnover experienced in healthcare over the past three years have made frontline clinical leadership roles very demanding. The approach to work among the professional clinical staff has changed, as discussed in Chapter 1, and these changes have impacted the role of frontline leaders. Steve's organization is now moving toward a team-based model of care and incorporating a clinical leader role. Steve realizes this will mean changes to his position and a need to develop new competencies.

New Leader Competencies

Like Steve, Kelsey has had to change her leadership practices. She manages a busy NICU. Kelsey was once a big believer that a nurse should spend two years on a unit before they were allowed to transfer. For many years, she could enforce this expectation but not today. She distinctly remembers the first interview just before COVID with a new graduate nurse when she talked about this, and he said – "*You are kidding.*" Fast forward to today, where she is happy to get nurses who stay a year – this is now her goal. She has embraced the one-and-done philosophy but still promotes longevity. Kelsey makes the case in every interview for waiting a year, and then the nurse can be one and done. From there, she will do everything she can to help the nurse achieve their next goal. Sometimes this works, and sometimes it does not. Kelsey had to change her leadership. She now focuses on how this nurse could best contribute to the team in the year she is with them.

Kelsey is not alone in seeing this change among her team members. Today's nurse manager is more like an NCAA basketball coach. The NBA has a rule that new players must be at least 19 years old before becoming professionals. Most top high school players now go to college teams for one year and then to the NBA. This one-and-done trend has led to rapid team turnover and coaching strategy changes. Some NCAA coaches contend that the rule has massively disrupted teamwork and made the coaching position more challenging. Chapter 4 will look at the implications of leading in a teaming environment.

Embracing a one-and-done philosophy in nursing today means the leader accepts that young nurses want to advance in their careers. As a nurse leader, you have two choices – embrace this change in the workforce or dig your heels in and try to enforce a policy that will result in nurses leaving you and your organization. Nurses today want their leaders to be coaches who support their career advancement goals. The challenge with a one-and-done culture is that you must lead differently and quickly build trust and teamwork among staff. For organizations, retention efforts must move from the unit to the organizational level as nurses seek to develop their careers. For Kelsey, this required changing how she looked at her role. She now sees herself less as a nurse manager and more as a team coach who helps her team work together more effectively. In recognition of these new demands on leaders, Kelsey's organization is now examining her span of control and the type of support she needs today to accomplish the new expectations.

Nurse leader roles are evolving because younger generations have different expectations of their managers. Younger staff want their leaders to be less like traditional leaders and more like team coaches.[30] The new expectations of leaders are highlighted in Figure 4.

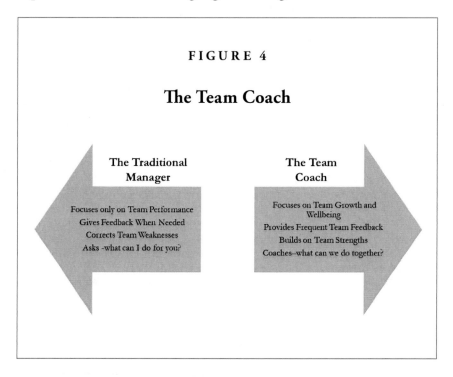

FIGURE 4

The Team Coach

The Traditional Manager

Focuses only on Team Performance
Gives Feedback When Needed
Corrects Team Weaknesses
Asks -what can I do for you?

The Team Coach

Focuses on Team Growth and Wellbeing
Provides Frequent Team Feedback
Builds on Team Strengths
Coaches—what can we do together?

TRANSITIONING TO THE ROLE OF TEAM COACH

Transitioning from being a traditional leader to a team coach is not always smooth. Jackson is a nurse manager in behavioral health. He always considered his leadership skills excellent, but now he is less confident. His younger staff seem to want more feedback and coaching than Jackson has ever done before. He has often asked himself whether he is still the right person to be in the role. He laughingly told a colleague that one of his new nurses came to him for career coaching after deciding that behavioral health is too stressful. Jackson is now working with her to look at other specialties that might better fit her strengths. In the past, he probably would not have taken the time to coach this young nurse who would eventually leave his team for other opportunities. He confides that he worries about his team's well-being because the behavioral health issues of hospitalized patients today are much more complex than in the past. Today much of his coaching does involve helping staff with their stress and anxiety management.

Coaching skills are now essential in any nursing leadership role, but coaching must be learned and practiced like any new competency. Most managers believe they are already good coaches, but the research suggests otherwise. When observed "coaching their staff" as part of research conducted by Harvard, the leaders were instead giving advice based on their own experiences.[31] This is not surprising. Nurse leaders are often selected for their positions because they are both great problem solvers and responsible for ensuring things get done. These are great strengths, but when you move into leadership, you must transition from being an individual performer to a team coach who gets work done through others. To effectively do this, leaders must be less like Superman and more like Yoda.[32]

When you use the Superman approach to leading, you swoop in and fix problems, usually receiving great feedback from staff about how responsive you are. Your door is always open, and you spend most of your day putting out fires as others bring them to your attention. You begin to find it hard to finish your administrative work because you are so available. Over time, this can lead to leadership burnout. You become indispensable, and your team members do not develop problem-solving abilities. Adrienne finds herself in this situation in her role as a dialysis manager. The dialysis unit is small, and Adrienne often takes patient assignments. She does her administrative work on the weekends, leaving little time to recharge her batteries. After a two-week vacation over the Christmas holidays, Adrienne returned and learned from the leader who covered the unit that the team "imploded" and was on the phone asking for guidance and help every day. Her colleague told Adrienne that she had not empowered the team and they were too reliant on her.

Adrienne knows her colleague is right. A better approach for her is to be more Yoda in her leadership. The Yoda is there to coach and support the team but will not solve all their problems. The Yoda is okay with things not being done their way and recognizes that mistakes will be part of the learning. When confronted with issues brought to them by staff, the Yoda asks questions that point the team in the right direction but does not give them the solution. The Yoda leader can take a day off and not receive 50 texts from staff about what is happening in the unit. The Yoda recognizes that they should not be indispensable or believe no department member could take their place if they left. Adrienne must develop her coaching skills with her team to facilitate this change. To begin to empower staff, she will also want to modify her behavior by doing the following:

- Set firmer boundaries between her work and home life to provide herself with a better work-life balance. No one can do this for her in her leadership role.
- Discuss with her staff what issues and problems she needs to be informed about when off duty and what issues and problems they should try to solve without her input.
- Close her office door at scheduled times to do her administrative work, hang a sign noting that she is available for emergencies, and then be clear about the definition of an emergency.
- Avoid solving team issues even if she can do it quickly and instead give guidance and ask questions such as, *What would you do if I was not here?* or *What do you think you should do next in this situation?*
- Accept that the staff's decisions may differ from how she would have managed a situation.
- Offer thoughtful and supportive feedback if she feels staff have made a mistake in their decisions and ask how they would manage it differently next time.

Being more Yoda will take extra time initially as Adrienne coaches the team, but the long-term payoff can be significant. The sign of a good leader who empowers their team is being able to take time off and trust that things will work smoothly.

DEVELOPING A COACHING MINDSET

In assuming the role of team coach, you must first adopt a coaching mindset. A coaching mindset means moving from a leadership style focused on fixing team weaknesses to a strengths-based approach focused on helping the team accelerate their professional growth through real-time feedback and communication. As we will discuss throughout this book, there are many situations where teams need coaching from their leaders. These include but are not limited to the following:

- Building strong team connections
- Valuing team diversity
- Delegating and assigning patient care
- Accepting shared accountability for patient care
- Providing strong team backup
- Promoting more effective teamwork
- Managing team relationships
- Dealing with team conflict
- Celebrating team achievements
- Establishing healthy team cultures
- Promoting team well-being
- Fostering team critical-thinking and problem-solving
- Communicating effectively as a team
- Utilizing team resources
- Collaborating with other areas and departments

Team coaching is a collaborative relationship undertaken between the coach and the team. It uses conversations to help the team plan and achieve its goals, enabling higher performance. Moving from being the problem solver-in-chief who tells others what to do to a coach takes practice. Listening, reflecting on what you hear and sense, and then asking powerful questions can change how a team sees themselves and their world.

In envisioning your role as the team coach, thinking about your experiences working or playing on a great team can be helpful. What did the leader do to facilitate the team's performance and help everyone to bring their best to the team's efforts? Shondra thought about this when she transitioned to the role of quality manager. She had played on a championship high school basketball team. She remembers her coach as a fantastic person who brought out the best in every player. The top eight things her coach did for the group included the following:

1. She made everyone feel safe and essential.
2. She trusted everyone and listened to our feedback.
3. She explained our roles and how we contributed to overall team efforts.
4. She always assumed good intentions in every situation and did not accuse or criticize.
5. She expected everyone's best performance, and we consistently exceeded her expectations.
6. She was not afraid to give straight feedback and tell hard truths.
7. She expected everyone to work as a team and did not tolerate drama.
8. She cared about us as human beings and not just as players.

These are the qualities that Shondra wants to emulate in her team leadership. She knows from reading about coaching that the key to being a great team coach is asking good questions. During her first three months in her role, she met one-on-one with each of her new quality management team members. To learn more about what was happening on the team before she began coaching, she asked the following questions:

- What is working well on the team?
- What things would you like to see changed to improve teamwork?
- What do you need from me as your team coach?
- How do you think I can be most effective in leading this team?
- What are you worried I might do as the leader of this team?

In this pre-assessment phase, Shondra learned some critical things about the team. One of their challenges was that although they worked in similar roles on the team, there was little communication within the group. Teamwork among the staff was not a core value. Every case manager covered their areas, did their work, and shared little about the challenges they were seeing. Their former manager had been punitive when there were errors, so Shondra's team worried she would lead with what they described as a "gotcha" style. Through her conversations, she realized there was little trust among team members. Her first actions would need to be around rebuilding trust and psychological safety.

A FRAMEWORK FOR COACHING

To become an effective team coach, leaders like Shondra also need to draw from best practices in coaching. One of the most widely used coaching models is the GROW Model, developed by Sir John Whitman and depicted in Figure 5.[33]

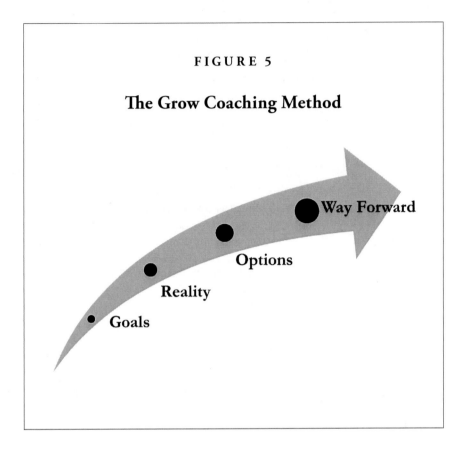

FIGURE 5

The Grow Coaching Method

Way Forward

Options

Reality

Goals

1. GROW – ESTABLISH TEAM GOALS.

The first step in the coaching process is to establish team goals. Shondra identified the team's lack of trust and psychological safety as significant challenges. In Chapter 6, we will discuss why it will be difficult for the team to move forward without trust and psychological safety as a foundation. Shondra will want to talk with the team about what she learned from her conversations with team members. To build trust and psychological safety, the team needs a written plan formalized with dates/times/activities. Some questions she could ask to establish team goals include the following:

- What do we want our team culture to be?
- What do we value the most in our work together?
- What team practices should we have that we don't have now?
- How would our ideal team function?

2. Reality – examine where the team is currently.

Too often, leaders try to solve a problem or reach a goal without fully considering their starting point. They may be missing the information they need to achieve their goals. Defining the current reality is essential. Shondra will want to share her observations and why re-establishing trust and safety is vital for team progress. She will also need input from the team. Some good coaching questions to ask in this phase include the following:

- How would you rate our current teamwork on a scale of one to ten?
- What would we want that rating of teamwork to be?
- What can we do to promote psychological safety for our team members?
- What obstacles stand in the way of us achieving better teamwork?

3. Options – explore ways to meet the goals.

Shondra can share her ideas about rebuilding team trust, but there must be a mutual commitment to act. Some questions to ask at this point include the following:

- What are some strategies that you would recommend to achieve the goals?
- Are there others outside the team who could help to provide insight and guidance?
- What might team members need to stop doing to be more successful?

- To promote trust and safety, what actions must we take as individuals?

4. Way Forward – identify what the team will do next.
The last coaching phase is where the work to meet the goals begins and where coaching feedback is provided. If the team decided to do the psychological safety assessment discussed in Chapter 6, it could be repeated over time to assess improvement. During this phase, the team coach and members can recommend changes and provide input on the plan's success. The feedback loop is an essential part of the coaching process. Coaching is not one-and-done – it is ongoing. Some questions Shondra can ask the team about the next steps include the following:

- What should our first action be to achieve these goals?
- How will we know if we are successful?
- How can we hold ourselves accountable to these goals?

Mastering Communication with a Team

Shondra knows that effective communication is one area where her team needs help. Research done at MIT indicates that the most important predictor of a team's success is communication patterns within the group.[34] In Chapter 8, we will discuss strategies to improve communication among team members. As a leader, Shondra will need to role model her communication expectations. A challenge for leaders is that there is a wide variety of communication styles and preferences with diverse teams. The most effective leaders know their preferred communication style and can flex it to meet their team members' needs.

Figure 6 outlines the four dominant communication styles researched initially by Dr. Tony Alessandra.[35] When you know your preferred style, you can work on adaptability. Flexing your style doesn't mean foregoing who you are but rather working toward being a better collaborator through recognizing the needs of others. Catherine, the nurse manager of a surgery unit, took the communication style inventory as part of a leadership program and realized that her dominant communication style was that of a director. When she first became a manager, this caused problems with her team as many of them were relators. Catherine was driven to get things done and did not take the time to develop more personal relationships with her team members. They commented on an employee satisfaction survey that she was unapproachable and uncaring.

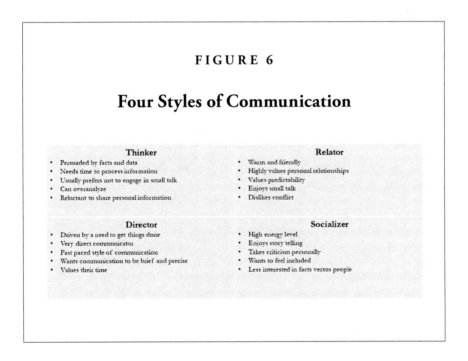

FIGURE 6

Four Styles of Communication

Thinker	Relator
• Persuaded by facts and data	• Warm and friendly
• Needs time to process information	• Highly values personal relationships
• Usually prefers not to engage in small talk	• Values predictability
• Can overanalyze	• Enjoys small talk
• Reluctant to share personal information	• Dislikes conflict

Director	Socializer
• Driven by a need to get things done	• High energy level
• Very direct communicator	• Enjoys story telling
• Fast paced style of communication	• Takes criticism personally
• Wants communication to be brief and precise	• Wants to feel included
• Values their time	• Less interested in facts versus people

After taking the leadership program, Catherine talked with her team about communication styles, including her own. She discussed the need for all team members to understand their communication styles and those of other team members. Catherine explained that it was never her intent to come across as unapproachable but understood how others might see her this way if their style differed. She vowed to work on flexing her communication style and encouraged her team to hold her accountable for her leadership communication goals.

Tailoring Team Leadership to Meet Generational Needs

As Catherine realized in her role, communication is not a one-size-fits-all approach. Team members have different communication styles, and today's nursing teams include staff from four different generational cohorts. Giancarlo discovered this when he took a leadership role in an urgent care center. The majority of his staff are either Millennials or Generation Z nurses. Although email is the official method of communication for his health system, many of his younger team members prefer other methods of communication. Some wanted their information on the unit's Facebook® site, others wanted texts, and others wanted him to use phone apps like GroupMe or Slack. He often found himself texting his staff to let them know that the health system had sent out an important email they needed to read. The emojis he used were viewed differently by team members. He recently sent some of his staff a thumbs-up emoji and was later told it was a passive-aggressive message.

Even face-to-face communication could prove challenging. Giancarlo recalls a recent conversation with one of his younger team members. *I was updating one of my new graduates about a practice change. She kept looking at me with what I thought was a quizzical look, so I tried another explanation. She said," Say less," I felt very offended. After all, I was doing my job and didn't expect a nurse to tell me to shut up. It turns out "say less" in Generation Z lingo means I get it. She was trying to say to me that she understood. Now I am learning that KEWL means cool, and CAP means you are lying, whereas No CAP means "for real" Who knew – now I have to relearn the language.*

Another area where Giancarlo sees generational differences is in ideas about the importance of teamwork. He is a Baby Boomer who grew up working on teams throughout his academic and professional career. Giancarlo has always had a team-first mindset in his nursing work. As he observed his new team, it surprised him how many didn't seem to value teamwork as he does. They want individual coaching from him and are reluctant to seek help from other team members. He had not considered that different generations might need different approaches from him as their leader while he sought to build a strong team.

Seasoned leaders like Giancarlo learn throughout their careers that the needs of staff change. An essential communication skill in meeting the needs of changing teams is to become a better listener. The best leaders understand that silence on teams is deadly and don't shut down conversations that don't conform to their worldview of what is happening. It is essential to always seek real-time information from your team. Some strategies to accomplish this include the following:

- Stay close to the team through leadership rounds, ask staff questions about their experiences, and include staff at all levels.
- Use this question often – What should I know is happening here but maybe don't?
- Ask the team if they have picked up additional responsibilities because of staffing shortages in other departments or supply chain issues.
- Stay silent for a moment after staff shares their viewpoints and then ask – And what else?
- Ask your team what you could do right now that would make their jobs easier.
- Ask other managers what trends they see with their unit's teams.
- Don't be defensive about what you hear – you may disagree, but continue to listen because there are often nuggets of truth in the feedback.

The best nurse leaders are learners seeking ways to communicate more effectively with their teams. Their never-ending pursuit of information pushes them to improve even when it is uncomfortable constantly. It is this practice that sets them apart from the rest.

KEY POINTS

✓ The turmoil, turbulence, and turnover experienced in health-care over the past three years have made frontline clinical leadership roles very demanding.

✓ Nurses today want their leaders to be coaches who support their career advancement goals.

✓ In assuming the role of team coach, you must first adopt a coaching mindset.

✓ The most effective leaders know their preferred communication style and can flex it to meet their team members' needs.

✓ An essential communication skill in meeting the needs of changing teams is to become a better listener.

CHAPTER 4

LEADING IN A TEAMING ENVIRONMENT

As discussed in Chapter 3, today's nurse leader role is more like an NCAA basketball coach who may see 50-100% of their roster rotate each year into the NBA. Future nursing teams will be more like airline crews who come together for short periods to achieve set goals. Healthcare has moved from core teams to *teaming*, a term coined by Harvard professor Amy Edmondson.[36] Unlike the traditional concept of core teams, teaming is an active process where interconnected individuals work on interdependent teams to achieve goals. The composition of a team in a teaming environment is fluid. Effective teaming requires members to listen to each other, coordinate their actions and participate in shared decision-making. Teaming is a dynamic activity and requires that members have a teamwork mindset. Figure 7 illustrates the differences between what happens on a traditional team versus a teaming environment.

FIGURE 7

A Move from Teams to Teaming

Teams	Teaming
• A stable group of nurses who work together for long periods of time.	• A dynamic group of nurses which shifts and changes over time.
• Members learn how to interact with each other and utilize each other's skills.	• Teamwork needs to be learned in real time.
• Seasoned members coach/mentor new nurses.	• Team members may all have little experience so new nurses will coach/mentor new nurses.
• Trust and communication are present from years of working together.	• Trust/communication and knowledge sharing needs to be quickly built with shifting teams.

Teams don't merge, take shape or strengthen independently, especially in a teaming environment. Edmondson points out that teamwork needs to be learned and requires strong leaders to promote a learning culture. The leader must foster a culture that builds the following behaviors:

- Asking good questions
- Sharing information
- Seeking help
- Being willing to experiment with unproven actions
- Talking about mistakes
- Seeking feedback

Four pillars drive success in a teaming environment.

1. **Speaking Up** – good teaming depends on honest, direct conversations among team members, including asking questions and giving feedback.

2. **Collaboration** – teaming requires a team mindset where teamwork is valued.
3. **Experimentation** – good teaming requires flexing, iterating, and changing if needed.
4. **Reflection** – teaming requires thoughtful questions and discussion of processes and outcomes.

THE LEADER AS FRAMER

Teaming environments are ones of significant change and sometimes turbulence. Your team members rely on you to explain the confusing signals often accompanying new initiatives or organizational changes. How the team thinks about what is happening in the environment frames the team behaviors that you see. Jason recently reflected on his experiences over the past few years framing the COVID experience and workforce turbulence in talking with his new graduate nurse team members in his critical care unit. They had asked him whether it would always be like this in healthcare. When he thought about their question, he realized the following:

- His young team had only worked in an ICU where everyone wore PPE, and expressions were hard to read.
- His young team had only worked in an ICU with a high census of COVID patients, where three to five patients died daily.
- His young team had only worked in an ICU where family visitation was prohibited.
- His young team had only worked in an ICU where they worried about getting sick themselves or bringing it home to their families.
- His young team had only worked in an ICU where staff did not socialize outside of work, and work rituals were suspended because of infection control requirements.

- His young team had only worked on teams where most RNs had limited experience, high turnover, and travel nurses were part of their core staffing.

Jason realized these young nurses were telling him they never thought nursing would be like this. They wondered why practice environments were in such turmoil. These conversations were difficult for Jason, but he spent much time discussing what was happening now and how things could look different in the future. Jason understands that those were dark days for his team, and his job is to help them to move through them. He often told his staff that he did not know precisely when this would end but was confident it would. Jason also reassured the team that they would emerge stronger due to their experience.

As Jason discussed initiatives with younger staff, he saw the importance of always beginning with the **why** behind any decision to gain buy-in. Simon Sinek advocates this approach of starting with **why** before moving to **how** or **what** is expected of the team.[37]

The Leadership Challenge

Nurse leaders like Jason have weathered some very challenging leadership situations over the past few years that tested their leadership. The movement to teaming and the loss of seasoned core nursing teams have been hard on leaders. As Jessie looked at the changes in her orthopedic nursing team, she knew some strategies and practices she used in the past no longer worked. She had to find a way to bring together a diverse staff that kept changing over time. Jessie struggled to find a leadership approach that would work and principles to guide her in this teaming environment. In a recent leadership development program, she learned about Kouzes and Posner's Exemplary Leadership ® Model. It seemed like a good fit to achieve the leadership needed in a teaming environment.

Jim Kouzes and Barry Posner's evidenced-based *The Five Practices of Exemplary Leadership Model* ® was developed using more than 40 years of research and assessments with 5 million leaders globally.[38] The authors believe that while the context of leadership changes over time, the content of leadership has not changed much, if at all. The five exemplary leadership practices in the model include: (a) *challenging the process,* (b) *inspiring a shared vision,* (c) *enabling others to act,* (d) *modeling the way, and* (e) *encouraging the heart.* A key finding is that teams want their leaders to be honest, forward-looking, competent, and inspiring. Based on their research, Kouzes and Posner identified five practices of exemplary leadership (Figure 8). Great leaders do the following for their teams:

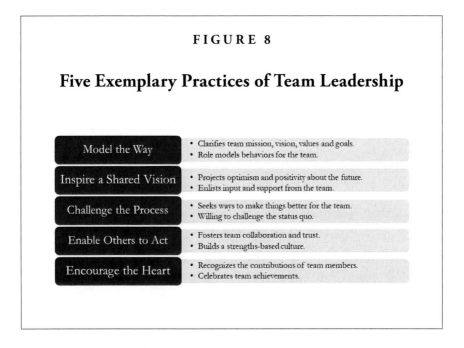

FIGURE 8

Five Exemplary Practices of Team Leadership

Model the Way	• Clarifies team mission, vision, values and goals. • Role models behaviors for the team.
Inspire a Shared Vision	• Projects optimism and positivity about the future. • Enlists input and support from the team.
Challenge the Process	• Seeks ways to make things better for the team. • Willing to challenge the status quo.
Enable Others to Act	• Fosters team collaboration and trust. • Builds a strengths-based culture.
Encourage the Heart	• Recognizes the contributions of team members. • Celebrates team achievements.

Modeling the way is fundamental because it is how leaders earn, sustain, and build credibility with the team. Effective leaders do what they say they will do. Before leaders can model the way, they must clarify their values. To do this, ask yourself questions such as:

- What do I believe in and use to make my decisions?
- What practices in my organization am I uncomfortable with? Have I been able to resolve my inner conflicts?
- What am I passionate about in my work?
- What is important to me when I recruit new team members?

The leader's values can be personal but must be congruent with the organization's. If your values conflict with your organization, it isn't easy to model the way effectively. A second key component to modeling the way is to ensure that your actions reflect your values. This behavior is known as "walking the talk." As a leader, you must set an example through your daily actions. If you are frequently late, counseling a team member about tardiness is difficult. Your team will watch the signals you send. Some effective behaviors to model the way include:

- Spend your time and job resources wisely.
- Watch the language you use, as words have power. Always talk about the "we versus I" and avoid words like "subordinates."
- Ask purposeful questions.
- Follow through on promises made.
- Seek feedback about your leadership.
- Confront critical incidents in a timely way.
- Repeat phrases that reflect the values that you want to build on your team.
- Use storytelling effectively to teach.
- Reinforce behaviors that you want to see repeated.

Inspiring a shared vision is essential in leadership because the team wants to work for leaders who look to the future with optimism and hope. The most effective leaders can imagine the possibilities of change and get others involved. They caution others about clinging to practices that are "sacred cows" but might not be suitable for the team's future.

They work hard to get the team on board with the new vision when there is a new direction. Staff wants to know that what they do matters and will continue to matter in the future. Leaders need to work hard to frame new visions in an easily understandable way. Before inspiring a shared vision, you must carefully evaluate your current behaviors. To do this, ask yourself the following questions:

- Do I react to change negatively?
- Do I carefully listen to the concerns of others or expect they will immediately adopt my vision?
- Do I think about the future and how it could impact our work?
- Am I positive, upbeat, and energetic about organizational changes, or do I convey disapproval?

No one wants to work with a leader who lives in the past and resists new changes. If you convey this behavior, it is impossible to inspire a shared vision.

In challenging the process, leaders should actively look for ways to improve, innovate and grow their teams. You must be willing to challenge the status quo to bring new methods, ideas, and solutions into use. In healthcare, we talk about the importance of evidence-based practice, but these changes often come slowly. Even when there is promising research about a need to change practices, widespread adoption can take several decades. Leaders are crucial in establishing cultures to challenge old processes and implement change. If you don't reward innovation, it will not become part of the culture. You must search for new opportunities and be willing to take risks. When you consider whether you promote challenging the process, ask yourself the following questions:

- How do I react when staff brings up a new way of doing something?
- How often do I say, "no, not now," or "we tried that once, and it did not work?"

- Am I current on the latest research and innovations in my field?
- How do I react when we implement new processes and staff don't follow through – do I accept it?
- Do I encourage initiative in others and seek suggestions from the team?

When enabling others to act, leaders recognize that success in any work requires a team effort. Leaders who enable others to act can foster collaboration and build team trust. They also allow others to do their best work by maximizing their strengths versus focusing on their weaknesses. You must be willing to share power and develop others to enable others. Research with younger staff indicates that leaders dedicated to developing others are much more successful in their recruitment and retention efforts.[37] A crucial role of any leader is to serve as a coach to help staff organize their work, build competence and accept accountability. Great leaders foster self-confidence by believing in their staff and offering choices about accomplishing work. When you consider whether you, as a leader, enable others, ask yourself the following questions:

- Do I recommend staff for educational development opportunities?
- Can I identify at least one staff member who could easily step into my role if I left the organization?
- How do I react when staff members leave the team for a growth opportunity?
- Do I trust staff to act in my absence, or do I question their decisions?
- Do I ask staff about their career goals and aspirations?

Encouraging the heart is the final exemplary practice in leadership. Leaders who encourage the heart seek to engage their team members by recognizing their unique contributions and who they are as individuals. It is essential to all of us that what we do matters and that our leaders will notice good work and be encouraging. Saying *thank you* may sound obvious, but it is often overlooked. A crucial part of encouraging the heart is recognizing contributions in a way valued by the person and celebrated by the team. Creating a sense of community in teams through celebrations is vital in building commitment and social support. Leaders must be present at these events to communicate their gratitude and send a strong message about the value of the contribution. When you consider whether you encourage the heart, ask yourself the following questions:

- Do I look for opportunities to celebrate team achievements, or do I convey an attitude that we are just doing our jobs?
- Am I personally present when team celebrations occur?
- How often do I thank you or send a message recognizing outstanding performance?
- Do I want to create community and social support in my work unit?

SEEKING HONEST FEEDBACK FROM THE TEAM

As Jessie went through her leadership development program, she learned that the only way she would know if she successfully implemented these five exemplary practices would be to seek feedback. Fortunately, her organization included a 360-degree leadership practices inventory (LPI) in the program.[39] Leadership assessments help us to gain insight into our leadership. Jessie's leadership was evaluated on 30 leadership behaviors documented as best practices in five exemplary areas. There were also five open-ended questions. Her supervisor, co-leader peers, direct reports, and observers from other departments completed the LPI assessment. The highest score she could achieve in any one practice area was 60.

Her scores ranged from a high of 47.8 in *Enabling Others to Act* to a low of 43.1 in *Challenging the Process*. Jessie was disappointed that her scores were not higher. She learned about her leadership strengths from the answers given to the open-ended questions. The feedback indicated staff saw her as having the following attributes:

- Creativity
- Caring leader
- Collaborative
- Positive and approachable
- A visionary with lots of ideas
- Calm and friendly
- Transparent communicator

She also learned about some key opportunities for improvement in her leadership, which included the following:

1. Focus on a more limited number of goals and provide more structure about accomplishing them.
2. Be sure to follow up on commitments and close the loop on problems.
3. Look for opportunities to delegate work to grow your staff.
4. Seek more feedback about your performance and make sure your self-perceptions are congruent with how others see you.

Jessie shared the findings with her team and began by thanking them for their feedback. The 360-degree assessment was the first time she had received such direct staff feedback. The input provided significant insight into how others view her behavior. The late Norman Vincent Peale once observed that *the trouble with most of us is that we would rather be ruined by praise than saved by criticism.*[40] This can quickly happen in leadership because the higher you go, the less likely you will get honest feedback.

Getting honest feedback can be very challenging. Staff may be fearful if they think the leader will retaliate, and they might jeopardize their careers. Leadership expert Ken Blanchard has described feedback as the breakfast of champions, but many nurse leaders will tell you that it can be difficult to swallow.[41] You may not have the opportunity to use a 360-degree leadership assessment, but three good questions to ask your team to get specific feedback include the following:

1. What should I **start doing** as a leader to work more effectively with the team?
2. What should I **stop doing** as a leader because it gets in the way of great teamwork?
3. What should I **continue doing** as a leader because it brings out the best in our team?

The value of these questions is that they are specific in eliciting the type of feedback you need in your leadership and are open-ended, and can't be answered with a yes or no. Don't just ask team members with whom you have good relationships. Engaging in conversations with those who may disagree with your viewpoints is especially important. Listen, and don't be defensive. You won't agree with all your feedback but look at recurring themes, patterns, and messages. Chapter 7 will discuss the importance of a team culture of professional feedback. As the leader, you need to role model the acceptance of feedback. The most effective leaders are coachable. While positive feedback is wonderful, much of our most significant growth will come with suggestions to improve our performance.

KEY POINTS

✓ Future nursing teams will be more like airline crews who come together for short periods to achieve set goals.

✓ Teaming must be learned and requires strong leaders to promote a learning culture.

✓ Your team relies on you to frame the confusing signals often accompanying new initiatives or organizational changes.

✓ Jim Kouzes and Barry Posner's evidenced-based *The Five Practices of Exemplary Leadership Model*® was developed using more than 40 years of research and assessments with 5 million leaders globally

✓ The most effective leaders are coachable. While positive feedback is wonderful, much of our most significant growth will come with suggestions to improve our performance.

CHAPTER 5

TEACHING NURSES TO LEAD TEAMS

In team-based delivery models, care is designed around the patient to ensure that those with the most expertise for particular needs are involved with patient care. Instead of one nurse with a designated patient load, a nurse-led team works together to care for a group of patients. Team models require a shift in mindset from "I" to "we." Rather than thinking, "I will do x for this patient today," change to "We will do x for these patients today," and define who will be responsible for each of those actions.

The transition to nurse-led teams can be challenging. Bob, an acute care service line director, volunteered his units to pilot a new collaborative care model. The RNs in medical-surgical nursing would be clinical leaders in a new care model that included patient care technicians, LPNs, and exercise physiologists who would help ambulate patients. Given how challenging it had been to staff the areas, Bob and the unit managers thought the staff would be excited about the pilot project. As he talked about clinical leadership, one of the RNs said, *"We are nurses, not leaders- that's the manager's job."* He wondered how the service line would ever be able to move to a team or collaborative care model if nurses didn't see themselves as leaders. Bob realized that the nurses needed a leadership mindset before developing the competencies required. He also discovered three types of nurses in his service line:

- Nurses who don't want to lead the team.
- Nurses who want to lead the team but shouldn't.
- Nurses who want to lead the team and should lead the team.

Changing the narrative nurses have about themselves as leaders involves changing mindsets. The first and most challenging step is to move nurses from the "fixed" mindset of seeing leadership as a role to a "growth" mindset of seeing leadership as the power to influence and work with others. Dr. Carol Dweck, a researcher and professor at Stanford University, pioneered studying how transformative a growth mindset can be for individuals. A *mindset,* according to Dweck, is a self-perception or "self-theory" that people hold about themselves. Mindsets can either be growth-oriented or fixed.[42] With a growth mindset, the nurses in Bob's service line would believe that they can lead and influence others on the team. With a fixed mindset, they would see leadership as a formal role with staff directly reporting to you. For those with a fixed mindset about leadership, you can't be a leader without a formal role.

To foster a leadership mindset, Bob realized that he and the managers would need to begin coaching nurses differently and move them from an inward focus on their work to an outward focus on what was happening with the team and unit. He put together a planning team that developed a three-bucket approach using the focus areas of **Leading Self, Leading Others, and Leading in the Organization** to develop the team leaders as outlined in Figure 9.

FIGURE 9

The Three-Bucket Approach to Team Leader Development

Bucket	Key Content Areas
Leading Self	• Developing a leadership mindset. Moving from an individual performer to a team leader. • Understanding your strengths. • Assessing your emotional intelligence. • Building trust and authenticity. • Knowing your leadership voice. • Honing your decision-making skills. • Seeking feedback on your leadership. • Reflecting on your successes and setbacks. • Understanding your communication style.
Leading Others	• Building cohesive teams. • Delegating and supervising care. • Establishing communication pathways with your team. • Building psychological safety on the team. • Giving effective feedback and holding staff accountable. • Promoting constructive conflict. • Giving meaningful recognition. • Promoting team engagement and shared governance. • Managing team resistance to change. • Fostering team well-being and resilience.
Leading in the Organization	• Understanding organizational policies and procedures. • Reviewing job descriptions for responsibilities and scope of practice for team members. • Managing team resources. • Fostering a team culture of safety and quality. • Understanding performance metrics. • Collaborating with other teams.

THE FIVE VOICES OF TEAM LEADERSHIP

As part of developing a leadership mindset, Bob felt it was essential that the future clinical leaders gain insight into their leadership voice and how others on the team would view their communication and behavior. The planning team selected *The Five Voices of Leadership as the assessment framework they would use in team leadership development.*[43] Built on the work of Karl Jung, the underlying belief is that every voice is equally important to the group dynamic, yet as leaders, certain voices tend to get the most airtime. The most charismatic can inspire everyone to follow their vision. Still, they can also become overbearing and unintentionally aggressive, often drowning out the quieter voices at the expense of relationships and great ideas. Each of us has a foundational leadership voice that comes naturally to us and will usually be our default voice when stressed. The clinical leaders in his program identified their foundational voice from an assessment and sought input from others about whether they accurately viewed their leadership behaviors. They also learned in what situations they may need to flex from their natural voice. Figure 10 illustrates the five voices.

FIGURE 10

Five Voices of Team Leadership

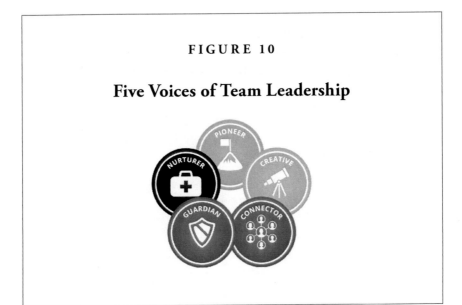

Most clinical leaders in the program (45%) identified **nurturer** as their foundational voice when working on teams. Nurturers are champions of relational harmony and are naturally wired to put the needs of others above their own. They bring some essential benefits to a team, such as:

- They have high social awareness about how the team is doing.
- They are relational and put people first.
- They naturally celebrate the achievements of others and are team players.

The second most common voice among the clinical leaders was **the guardian** (29%). Guardians guard, protect and defend values, systems, and discipline. Their strengths on the team include:

- They are willing to ask difficult questions.
- They honor the past and understand why things are done in specific ways.
- They are accountable and responsible.
- They respect and value policies and procedures.

A smaller number of clinical leaders (12%) identified their leadership voice as **creative**. Creatives are futurists. Of all the voices, they probably would be the most likely group to support a change in care delivery. They believe you can always find a way to solve problems and are willing to think outside the box. The strengths they bring to the team include the following:

- They are early adopters of change, believing things can always be better.
- They function as an 'early warning radar system' for teams, often seeing opportunities and dangers long before everyone else.
- If the vision is compelling, the word 'can't' is not in their vocabulary.

- They exhibit a strong social conscience and desire for personal and organizational integrity.

Ten percent of the clinical leaders identified **connector** as their foundational voice. Connectors are natural people pleasers who value relationships and helping others. Connectors benefit their teams by doing the following:

- They are inclusive and quick to embrace new team members.
- They are incredibly resourceful and know how to accomplish things in the organization.
- They help teams develop rituals and establish a sense of community.
- They know how to connect with people and their aspirations.

The smallest percentage of the clinical leaders (4%) identified **pioneer** as their foundational voice. Pioneers love to move forward into the future and accomplish significant initiatives. They can be competitive and inspirational but also overbearing. Pioneers contribute to teams by doing the following:

- They have a can-do attitude.
- They are very strategic in how to get things done.
- They can effectively align the team toward achieving goals.
- They are powerful communicators.

Understanding their foundational leadership voice proved helpful for the clinical leaders as they developed their team leadership skills. Having insight into their preferred voice can help avoid the pitfalls of their default style. If your foundational voice is that of a nurturer, you are probably far less likely to want to engage in conflict. If you do, you will likely be accommodating to the needs of others, whether or not it is the right strategy in the situation. If your foundational voice is either the pioneer or guardian, you might take a competing stance in a conflict making it difficult to come to any resolution. Creatives, connectors, and nurturers may naturally default to compromise versus collaboration. The clinical leaders learned that in leadership, the most challenging person you will ever lead is you. Excellent team leadership starts with self-leadership.

SUPERVISION AND DELEGATION OF CARE

Katie recently added licensed practical nurses (LPNs) and patient care technicians(PCTs) to her mother-baby unit teams. The initial transition had been rocky as most of her staff had little experience supervising and delegating care. The RNs worried about placing their nursing licenses in jeopardy. While many had served in charge nurse roles, assigning care to other RNs, most had not supervised or delegated care to non-RN team members. The ability to delegate, assign and supervise care are critical competencies for every RN, especially those who work in team-based care delivery systems. The decision of whether or not to delegate or assign care to a team member is based on the RN's judgment concerning the condition of the patient, the competency of the team member, and the degree of supervision needed if care is delegated.[44]

Decisions about what care can be delegated have multiple decision points. Individual states have practice acts and statutes about the role and scope of practice of healthcare team members that must be followed. The hospital or health system must develop policies and procedures about what responsibilities can be delegated, to whom, and under what circumstances. The RN is responsible for assessing patient needs and then delegating care based on the competencies of staff members. The staff member to whom care is entrusted is accountable for ensuring they have the competency for the delegated responsibility and following up with the nurse who supervises the care.

When Katie's unit transitioned to including LPNs and PCTs on the nursing team, she found that many RNs did not understand the scope of practice of the LPN role. Some were reluctant to delegate care appropriate to the LPN position descriptions; others saw little difference between the RN and LPN roles and delegated aspects of care that should not have been delegated. She realized teaching nurses about supervision and delegation was not a one-and-done activity. As the leader, she would need to ensure that the RNs read the hospital policies and the position descriptions of all healthcare team members. As new nurses join the unit, this must also be included in hospital and unit orientation for new staff members.

Katie found with her team that using assignment case scenarios helped the nurses understand and critically think through the following five rights of delegation:[44]

The right task: The activity falls within the staff member's job description or is included in the established written policies and procedures of the nursing practice setting. The facility needs to ensure the policies and procedures describe the expectations and limits of the activity and provide any necessary competency training.

The right circumstance: The health condition of the patient must be considered. If the patient's condition becomes unstable, the staff member must communicate this to the RN, and the RN must reassess the situation and the appropriateness of the delegation.

The right person: The RN delegating care must ensure that when assigning care, the staff member possesses the appropriate skills and knowledge to perform the activity. It must also be within their scope of practice.

The right directions and communication: Each delegation situation should be specific to the patient, the RN, and the staff member to whom care is delegated. The RN should communicate specific instructions for the delegated activity. This communication includes any data that must be collected, the data collection method, the time frame for reporting the results to the RN, and additional information pertinent to the situation.

The right supervision and evaluation: The RN is responsible for monitoring the delegated activity, following up with the team member after the activity, and evaluating patient outcomes. The RN should also ensure appropriate documentation of care given.

Katie realized that successfully transitioning to a team approach to care would take vigilance and follow-up. As part of the reboot, she instituted a mid-shift huddle on the unit. This additional huddle enhanced team communication, sometimes leading to assignment revisions and identifying high-risk patients.

RELATIONSHIP MANAGEMENT

Few nursing graduates have received education about leading teams over the past three decades. Moving from being an individual contributor to leading a team is a transition. Leadership is both an art and a science. While understanding supervision and delegation is essential, managing relationships with other team members is equally important. Chelsey's unit was moving to a team-based approach to care. Nurses assuming the role of team leader had attended leadership classes. Maura was a unit team leader, although she was reluctant to take on the responsibilities. Chelsey watched Maura during the shift huddle and was concerned about the behaviors that she observed. She knew that cohesive teams have three key ingredients: safety, belonging, and mattering.[45] One of the patient care technicians had asked whether a patient should be reclassified to a fall risk based on his experiences caring for him the day before. Maura responded abruptly, *"Patient assessment is my responsibility, not yours."*

Chelsey knows from the research that engaging team members are vital to teamwork, yet RNs and UAPs have different mental models about their respective roles, which impact relationships and communication.[46] When RNs don't include a PCT in decision-making, they will feel devalued and diminished, which could affect their future willingness to be team players.[47] It also leads to less ownership of the goals of the team, unit, and organization. Ultimately it is also a patient safety issue as the PCT is unlikely to voice future patient safety concerns. Chelsey knows Maura is new to leadership, so she plans a structured feedback session to deliver the message about managing relationships on teams yet avoiding the drama that sometimes accompanies negative feedback. She uses the Center for Creative Leaders SBI (situation-behavior-impact) model.[48]

Situation – Describe the context of the situation along with the details of what happened and when. Chelsey might say – *"At shift huddle this morning, I observed that Mike asked whether one of the patients on your team should be assigned as a fall risk. He had cared for the patient yesterday."*

Behavior – Describe what happened and what was observed in a fact-based and judgment-free manner. Chelsey might say – *"Your response to Mike was that patient assessment is your responsibility, not his. While true, he had some valuable information about the patient to contribute."*

Impact – Explain the effect of the behavior and why it is an issue with potentially adverse outcomes. Chelsey might say – *"It may not have been your intent, but this behavior impacts team morale and demoralizes Mile. It is a patient safety issue because Mike may be less inclined to report things to you if he worries about your negative reaction."*

Chelsey will want to seek Maura's response to what is said. The value of the SBI framework is that it removes character criticisms from the conversation. Instead, you evaluate actions within a specific context while explaining why those actions might not result in the best outcomes.[49] When giving feedback, it can be helpful to have some guiding questions to use in the conversation to clarify the nurse's viewpoint on relationship management with the rest of the team. Some examples include:

- What don't I know about this situation?
- What could you have done differently in this situation?
- How would you handle this situation differently in the future?
- How can we fix this?

Chelsey needs to be clear in the feedback that she is giving. Leaders sometimes use the compliment sandwich. They start with a compliment, put the feedback in the middle, and then end with a compliment. While this can be the right approach in some situations, it is usually best to get to the point. Chelsey should let Maura know that she needs to share feedback to help Maura grow in her leadership. The input she is giving may be challenging to hear but is important.[49]

The next phase of the conversation is a discussion about future expectations. Chelsey should acknowledge Maura's value to the team and convey the aspects of professional behavior that need to change to improve relationship management. She could then work with the nurse to establish a plan, including a conversation with Mike, the PCT. It will be important that when improvement does happen, it is acknowledged and reinforced. Learning to navigate team relationships successfully will be an ongoing journey for every RN team leader.

Using Team Resources

While accountability for the budget is generally not the responsibility of the team leader, the wise use of team resources is vital. There are two key areas to include in team leader training. The first involves the use of supplies and equipment. Team members are often unaware of equipment and supply costs in their inpatient or outpatient settings. Medical supplies account for up to 17 percent of total hospital expenses.[50] Reducing supply use can have a significant impact on a unit budget. Excessive use of supplies or a failure to scan supplies can quickly add up and impact a unit or department's budget. Likewise, when supplies and equipment are not readily available, excessive team time is spent on "hunting and gathering" activities. Teams need to report problems and not do workarounds.

Ray, a manager in radiology, was having challenges getting the supply budget under control. He thought that with some team education, they could bring costs down. Ray decided to make learning fun by holding his own *The Price is Right* contest and awarding prizes to staff who came closest to guessing the costs of the ten most commonly used supplies in his area. His team was shocked at the actual prices, and most did not come close in their guessing. This contest set the stage for a practical brainstorming session about lowering costs. One of his staff members suggested placing a supply drop box on the unit with the reminder to empty your pockets before leaving. He was surprised at how many supplies the staff had in their pockets at the end of the shift that they might have taken home without the reminder.

A second key area to include in team leader training involves the cost and utilization of human capital. When units and departments have budget overruns, it is usually the result of staffing decisions. A team approach to care delivery changes the staffing and skill mix. There is no magic formula to determine the right staffing and skill mix. The following are five qualitative factors in any organization or on any unit that also need to be considered:[51]

1. The organization and work rules - The type of organization can make a difference. Team staffing needs may differ in academic settings where team members work closely with house staff to coordinate care versus in a community hospital with a stable hospitalist group. Some organizations establish work rules that impact scheduling, such as the number of hours a team member can work consecutively or weekends off each month.

2. The patient population - Units or organizations with a higher case mix of older patients may require different staffing than organizations with a younger population, even with the same patient acuity. Some patient populations are at higher risk for falls, infections, and pressure ulcers. Expectations about team involvement in discharge planning also need to be considered.

3. Support services and architectural layout – The level of ancillary support to the organization's team will impact the staffing needs. Are team members expected to answer the phone and transport patients? The geographical layout of a unit can make the work of team members either easier or more demanding. Patients today expect private rooms, but depending on the features and design of those rooms – it may increase the team's work and make communication more challenging.

4. Daily census and unit turnover - Much team time today is spent on admissions, transfers, and discharges. The volume of these activities is often not reflected in a patient census taken once a shift.

5. Staff expertise and competence – Team member expertise and competence must be considered when staffing a unit. Departments with a higher percentage of novice team members may need more staffing.

Team leaders play an essential role in helping to manage team overtime and recommending cost-effective ways to cover gaps in the schedule. When Jackie assumed an emergency department (ED) director position, she examined her budget overruns and found several ways she could coach team leaders to lower staffing costs. They included the following:

- Team members clocked out 15 minutes after their shift to finish their documentation and manage other team-related patient care issues resulting in thousands of dollars in overtime each month.
- Team leaders made no mid-shift staffing adjustments to accommodate an increase or decrease in patient volumes resulting in staffing variances.

- When staffing was short, the default plan was to call in agency RNs, which cost the facility more money than EMTs, per diems, or staff working overtime.
- ED nurses were assigned as sitters in the ED for patients who had overdosed instead of seeking EMTs or PCT team members who could cover these responsibilities.

Jackie's findings are not unusual. When team resources are not closely monitored, expenses increase, and productivity declines. There are no easy solutions to team staffing problems, and the answers may not be universal. In today's healthcare environment, managing team productivity is a delicate balance between meeting the patient's needs for care and maintaining fiscal responsibility.

KEY POINTS

- ✓ Great team leadership starts with self-leadership.
- ✓ Team models require a shift in mindset from "I" to "we."
- ✓ Decisions about care delegation have multiple decision points.
- ✓ Learning to navigate team relationships successfully will be an ongoing journey for every RN team leader.
- ✓ Team leaders play an essential role in helping to manage team overtime and recommending cost-effective ways to cover gaps in the schedule.

References

1. Feiler B. Life is in the Transitions: Mastering Change at an Age. New York: Penguin Press; 2020.
2. Hoffman R, Casnocha B, Yeh C. Tours of duty: The new employer-employee contract. *Harvard Business Review June 2013.* Available at https://hbr.org/2013/06/tours-of-duty-the-new-employer-employee-compact
3. Smiley RA, Ruttinger C, Oliveira CM, et al. The 2020 National Nursing Workforce survey. *Journal of Nursing Regulation.* 2021;12(1): S1-S96. Available at https://www.sciencedirect.com/science/article/pii/S2155825621000272
4. HHS (May 2022). New Surgeon General Advisory Sounds Alarm on Health Worker Burnout and Resignation. Available at https://www.hhs.gov/about/news/2022/05/23/new-surgeon-general-advisory-sounds-alarm-on-health-worker-burnout-and-resignation.html
5. 2022 NSI National Health Care Retention & RN Staffing Report. Available at https://www.nsinursingsolutions.com/Documents/Library/NSI_National_Health_Care_Retention_Report.pdf.
6. ANA Workplace Pulse Survey (July 2022). Available at https://www.nursingworld.org/practice-policy/work-environment/health-safety/disaster-preparedness/coronavirus/what-you-need-to-know/covid-19-survey-series-anf-2022-workplace-survey/
7. Vespa J, Medina L, Armstrong D. *Demographic Turning Points for the United States: Population Projections for 2020 to 2060;* Current Population Reports, U.S. Census Bureau. 2020.
8. Becker's Hospital Review (July 13th, 2022). CDC, CMS and others call for urgent action on patient safety. Available at https://www.beckershospitalreview.com/patient-safety-outcomes/cdc-cms-call-for-urgent-action-on-patient-safety.html
9. American Association of Critical Care Nurses (May 5th, 2022). National Nurse Staffing Think Tank Launched by Leading Health

Care Organizations Develops Solutions Tool Kit to Address Staffing Crisis. Available at https://www.aacn.org/newsroom/national-nurs e-staffing-think-tank-launched-by-leading-health-care-organizations

10. Incredible Health Webinar. (August 3, 2022). How Legacy hires and retains permanent nurses. Available at https://www.incredible-health.com/blog/employers/webinar/watch-how-legacy-health-hires-and-retains-permanent-nurses/

11. "Albert Einstein Quotes." BrainyQuote.com. BrainyMedia Inc, 2022. 4 September 2022. Available at https://www.brainyquote.com/quotes/albert_einstein_121993

12. Health Solutions Group (2023). Models of Care Insight Study. Available at https://healthcareplussg.com/models-of-care-insigh t-study-results/

13. AHA (November 2022 Brief). Measuring the value of team-based care: A dashboard for healthcare organizations. Available at file:///C:/Users/roseo/OneDrive/Documents/Book%20Team%20Nursing/issue-brief-measuring-the-value-of-team-based-care%20AHA.pdf

14. Griner T. Robotic Support of Nursing Care: State of the Technology and Future Predictions. *Nurse Leader.* 20(6). 569-573.

15. Poirer A. (January 12th, 2023). Trinity Health examines an in hospital virtual care model Available at https://grbj.com/news/health-care/trinity-health-examines-in-hospital-virtual-care-model/

16. Davis C. (HealthLeaders February 13, 2023). At Atrium Health, virtual nursing increases patient satisfaction, decreases falls and medication errors. Available at https://www.healthleadersmedia.com/nursing/exec-atrium-health-virtual-nursing-increases-patient-satisfa ction-decreases-falls-and

17. AONL Workforce Compendium Section 2 (2023) Available at https://www.aonl.org/system/files/media/file/2023/01/AONL_WorkforceCompendium2_final.pdf

18. Lambertsen E. *Education for nursing leadership.* Philadelphia: JB Lippincott, 1958.

19. Sherman RO. Team Nursing Revisited. *Journal of Nursing Administration.* 1990;20(11):43-46.

20. Covey SR. *The 7 Habits of Highly Effective People 30th Anniversary Edition.* New York: Simon & Schuster; 2020.

21. Wymer JA, Weberg DA, Stucky CH, Allbaugh NN. Human-Centered Design: Principles for Successful Leadership Across Health Care Teams and Technology. 2023; 21(1):91-96.

22. Health Care/System Redesign. Content last reviewed April 2022. Agency for Healthcare Research and Quality, Rockville, MD. Available at https://www.ahrq.gov/ncepcr/tools/redesign/index.html

23. AHQR 2019. Missed Nursing Care. Available at https://psnet.ahrq.gov/primer/missed-nursing-care

24. Institute for Healthcare Improvement. (ND) Clinical Microsystem Assessment Tools. Available at https://www.ihi.org/resources/Pages/Tools/ClinicalMicrosystemAssessmentTool.aspx

25. Institute for Healthcare Improvement. (ND). Plan-Do-Study-Act Worksheets. Available at https://www.ihi.org/resources/Pages/Tools/PlanDoStudyActWorksheet.aspx

26. Duhigg, C. *The Power of Habit: Why We do What We do in Life and Business.* New York: Random House; 2012.

27. Rogers E. *Diffusions of Innovation 5th Edition.* New York: Free Press; 2003.

28. Bunker K A. In Rush. S. (Editor) *On Leading in Times of Change.* Greensboro, N.C.: Center for Creative Leadership; 2012

29. AONL (August 2022). Longitudinal Nursing Leadership Insight Survey Part 4: Nurse Leader's Top Challenges and Areas for Needed Support. Available at https://www.aonl.org/resources/nursing-leadership-covid-19-survey

30. Clifton J, Harter J. *It's the Manager.* New York: Gallup Press; 2019.

31. Milner J, Milner T. (August 14th, 2018 HBR Blog). *Most Managers Don't Know How to Coach People. But They Can Learn.* Available

at https://hbr.org/2018/08/most-managers-dont-know-how-to-coach-people-but-they-can-learn

32. Raymond, J. (Interview Huffington Post April 27th, 2017 blog). Dear Boss: Be More like Yoda, Less Like Superman. Available at https://www.huffpost.com/entry/dear-boss-be-more-like-yoda-less-like-superman_b_590252a8e4b05279d4edba5e

33. Performance Consultants (updated 2022). The GROW coaching model. Available at https://www.performanceconsultants.com/grow-model

34. Pentland A. On Teams. Boston: Harvard Business Review Press; 2013.

35. Alessandra T, Alessandra A. *People Smart: Powerful Techniques for Turning Every Encounter into a Mutual Win.* Keynote Publishers; 1995.

36. Edmondson A. Teaming: How Organizations Learn, Innovate and Compete in the Knowledge Economy. San Francisco: Jossey-Bass; 2012.

37. Sinek S. *Start with Why: How Great Leaders Inspire Everyone to Take Action.* Canada: Portfolio Press; 2011.

38. Kouzes JM, Posner BZ. The Leadership Challenge 7th Edition. Hoboken NJ: Wiley; 2023.

39. Leadership Practices Inventory 360-degree assessment. Available at https://www.leadershipchallenge.com/lpileadershippracticesinventory

40. Norman Vincent Peale (ND). Available at https://www.brainyquote.com/quotes/norman_vincent_peale_109427

41. Blanchard K, Conly R. *Simple Truths of Leadership: 52 Ways to Be a Servant Leader and Build Trust.* Oakland CA: Berrett-Koehler Publishers; 2022.

42. Dweck C. *Mindset: The New Psychology of Success.* New York: Random House; 2006.

43. Kubicek J, Cockram S. *5 Voices: How to Communicate Effectively with Everyone You Lead.* Hoboken, NJ: Wiley Publishers.

44. ANA-NCSBN (April 2019). National guidelines for nursing delegation. Available at https://www.ncsbn.org/nursing-regulation/practice/delegation.page

45. Comaford C. *Power your Tribe.* New York: McGraw Hill; 2018.

46. Campbell AR, Kennerly S, Swanson M, Forbes T, Anderson T, Scott ES. Relational quality between the RN and Nursing Assistant. *Journal of Nursing Administration.* 2021; 51(9):461-467.

47. Kalisch B J. The impact of RN – UAP relationships on quality and safety. *Nursing Management.* 2011; 42(9): 16-22.

48. Gentry WA. *Be the Boss Everyone Wants to Work For: A Guide for New Leaders.* Oakland CA: Berrett-Koehler Publishers; 2016

49. Glazer R. *Elevate Your Team.* Simple Truths Publishers; 2023.

50. Cleveland Clinic QD Consult. Cutting the cost of supplies. Available at https://consultqd.clevelandclinic.org/cutting-the-cost-of-supplies/

51. ANA Principles for Nurse Staffing 2019 3rd Edition Available at https://www.nursingworld.org/practice-policy/nurse-staffing/

PART 2

THE NUTS AND BOLTS OF TEAMWORK

"A team is not a group of people who work together;
a team is a group of people who trust each other."

SIMON SINEK

CHAPTER 6

BUILDING A STRONG
TEAM FOUNDATION

High-performance work teams in any setting rarely occur naturally. The late Casey Stengel was the coach of the New York Yankees and held the record for the most world series ever won by a manager. He often told reporters that *"It's easy to get good players. Getting them to play together, that's the hard part."*[1] Most nurse leaders would agree with this observation. Yet, guiding team members to get past their day-to-day problems, conflicts, and communication issues toward the goal of working as a high-performance work team poses significant challenges. Healthcare teams are highly interdependent, so good teamwork is essential. A need for teamwork is especially true with new team-based models of care where everyone should work at the top of their scope of practice.

Before teams can work together effectively, there must be a foundation to help promote teamwork. Leaders have not always understood the impact of trust and psychological safety on teamwork. Google learned that hiring the best software engineers does not always lead to the best team synergy or outcomes. Google initially researched this area in 2011 as part of Project Aristotle.[2] Harvard researchers studied 180 Google teams and found that psychological safety and trust mattered more on teams than individual expertise. These findings are consistent with the work by Patrick Lencioni, who contends that the primary drivers of team dysfunction are an absence of trust and psychological safety.[3]

When Maya accepted a position as manager of an infusion team, she spent her first 100 days holding one-to-one sessions with each team member. She was surprised at the team's lack of trust and psychological safety. Team members were reticent in the information that they shared with her. There seemed to be a lack of transparency about the team's challenges. When she asked them to evaluate teamwork among the group, the average score was a two on a scale of one to five. Several on the team complained about how pervasive gossip was among team members. The lack of trust among the infusion team members was the elephant in the room that few seemed willing to discuss. Maya knows any attempts to build a higher-performance team must include restoring trust and psychological safety.

Trust on Teams

Trust in teams begins with vulnerability. While it may seem paradoxical, you need humility and courage to promote trust.[4] Team members who trust one another learn to admit their failures, weaknesses, and fears. Team members who trust one another are readily able to say things such as:[5]

- I was wrong.
- I need help.

- I am not sure.
- I made a mistake.
- You are better at this than I am.

A challenge with trust is that it builds over time. When there is rapid turnover on the team, it can be harder to achieve. Maya's team had a 25% turnover in six months. She should not be surprised that there is little trust. Maya knows she must role model the vulnerability she hopes her team will achieve. She will need to go first. She shares information about what she had learned from her meetings with staff. She demonstrates vulnerability by sharing the following:

- She admits she is a new leader and does not have all the answers.
- She needs the help and support of the team to rebuild teamwork.
- She is honest with the team about what is and is not in her circle of influence as a leader.
- She discusses establishing trust and psychological safety as crucial steps in resetting the unit culture.

Trust is both earned and given. To rebuild trust, the team needs to trust each other as individuals and be trustworthy in their actions as team members. Achieving trust in groups requires a commitment to the professional accountability and responsibility discussed in Chapter 10. As a team member, I need to know that you will do what you say you will do, that you will be honest and transparent in communication, and that there will be team backup if I need it. I also need to know that I will be respectfully and fairly treated. Maya knows that change will take time. Her infusion team lacks a team-first mindset. Team members need to rebuild personal connections. She will have to give the team kudos for all the small steps they take in the right direction.

One issue that Maya does need to address immediately with the team is the prevalence of negative gossip. Harmful or malicious gossip is like a virus that can take over and destroy a healthy work environment. It often starts with one or two staff who are the ringleaders of the negative comments but can quickly spread as it becomes normalized into the team culture. Newer team members may begin to participate to feel accepted. Sometimes the participation is passive when team members listen to the conversation without commenting or trying to stop it. Unsurprisingly, some privately held companies now have a three-strikes and you-are-out policy on gossip.

Maya put the topic of negative gossip on a team meeting agenda. She reminded the team that negative gossip is counter to everyone's success. Maya differentiated negative gossip from positive gossip by asking the team to give examples of both kinds of gossip that they have observed. She wondered how knowing a team member might gossip about you felt. She told them the negative gossip had gotten out of control, and she intended to promote a different team culture. Maya also set up a *Gossip Fine for Charity* program to enable staff to call out behaviors that will result in fines. Moving to a more trusting culture will be a journey for Maya's team, yet essential for a better future. Excellent or lousy team experiences can make staff more or less eager to be part of a team in the future. If she implements the abovementioned strategies, she will see a shift in the team culture and help build psychological safety.

Psychological Safety on Teams

Jasmine interviewed for a senior director position in a new organization. She was enthusiastic about the possibilities of promotion, but as the round of interviews progressed, she began to feel uncomfortable and psychologically unsafe. No one answered why the previous director resigned or seemed willing to discuss it. The team, who would be her peers, seemed guarded and often deferred questions to the chief nursing officer. Jasmine left the interview deflated. She thought they would offer her the position, but there were too many red flags. She is wise to recognize that working on a leadership team, by its nature, involves interpersonal risks. Because healthcare delivery is rarely scripted and many unexpected things happen, the leadership team must be able to ask questions, offer ideas and coordinate their actions in real-time.[6] Without psychological safety, this is unlikely to occur.

Jasmine's uneasy feeling was her brain quickly assessing the degree of psychological safety in a new environment and the team interactions. Dr. Amy Edmondson is an expert on psychological safety in the workplace. She defines it as the following: "psychological safety describes the individuals' perceptions about the consequences of interpersonal risk in their work environment." It consists of taken-for-granted beliefs about how others will respond when you put yourself on the line, such as asking a question, seeking feedback, reporting a mistake, or proposing a new idea. We weigh each potential action against a particular interpersonal climate, as in, *"If I do this here, will I be hurt, embarrassed, or criticized?"* Actions that might be unthinkable in one workgroup can be readily taken in another due to different beliefs about probable interpersonal consequences.[7]

Just like individuals assess the psychological safety of their environments, the same is true with teams. Timothy Clark describes a four-stage team psychological safety model (Figure 11).[8]

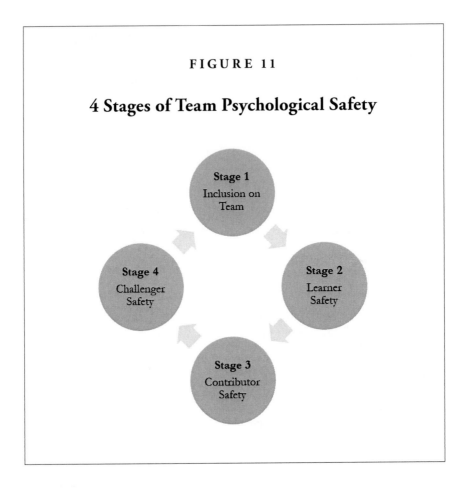

FIGURE 11

4 Stages of Team Psychological Safety

The first stage 1 is inclusion safety which is critical to psychological safety. When it is present, team members feel included, appreciated, and comfortable being part of the team. Stage 2 is learner safety. Team members feel like they can ask questions, and team members will provide support if needed. Stage 3 is contributor safety. Members feel they are valued and are not asked to do things they are not competent to do. The final stage is challenge safety, where members feel safe to raise tough issues and problems. If you assume a team leadership position and think psychological safety could be an issue in the culture, ask team members the following questions:[7]

1. If you make a mistake on this team, is it held against you?
2. Are you able to bring up problems and challenging issues?
3. Do people sometimes reject others for being different?
4. Is it safe to take a risk on this team?
5. Is it challenging to ask team members for help?
6. Do people on this team ever undermine your efforts?
7. Are your unique skills utilized and valued on this team?

On a team where staff feels psychological safety, staff has confidence that they will receive respect and consideration from others. A group with a culture of psychological safety encourages open discussion of challenging issues. It not only tolerates disagreement, but it also nurtures contrasting points of view. Team leaders can help create these environments by developing and reinforcing the following team behaviors:

- **Model Inclusion** – model inclusion for the team fosters psychological safety by including all team members in huddles and team rounding.

- **Argue with Respect** – demonstrate civility when navigating team conflicts and encourage tolerance of diverse points of view.

- **Provide Team Backup** – design team processes to make it easy to ask for help and an expectation that team members will provide it.

- **Recognize Gifts and Talents** – utilize the gifts and talents of team members.

- **Encourage Discussion of Tough Issues** – tackle challenging issues and thank the staff who dare to surface team problems.

Feeling safe on a team can increase a person's energy, enthusiasm, and zest for life. Team leaders who hold themselves and the team accountable to behavioral standards that improve psychological safety create robust and positive team cultures.

Team Values

Jake joined a hospice organization as a regional team leader. During his onboarding, he asked about his new team's values. His graduate leadership nursing studies taught him the importance of values and purpose in teamwork. By identifying the principles that matter most, the team can gain tremendous clarity and focus on making consistent decisions and taking action when needed.[9] Jake was surprised that his new team understood the purpose of their work but did not have any team values. Values should constitute the team's "bottom line" and tell members when to say no and when to say yes. The more explicit teams are about their values, the easier it will be to hold each other accountable.[10]

Jake decided to talk about team values at his first meeting and ask his team members what values they believed the team should have. At first, he was unsure they would ever gain consensus, but they did. They brainstormed as a group and identified seven core values that they would commit to:

1. Work collaboratively as a team.
2. Deliver exceptional team care to our hospice patients.
3. Assume good intentions about other team members.
4. Respect and value the diversity among team members.
5. Have a team-first mindset to provide team backup when needed.
6. Own our mistakes.
7. Find joy in our work.

Deciding on a set of team values was highly unifying to the team. Shared values give team members reasons to care about what they do and make a difference in work attitudes and performance. Jake realized that establishing these values could help set team priorities and navigate difficult times. Once the team agreed on the values, Jake made a plaque and posted it in their office. When interviewing new staff, Jake now looks for congruence between the team values and those of the person interviewed. When the team has complex staffing challenges or conflicts, Jake centers the team on their values as a point of agreement. Everyone is accountable for upholding the team's values.

ROLE CLARITY

Healthcare has been described as a team sport because each discipline and staff member's contributions to patient care are interdependent. In their training, most nurses are socialized into their profession but may have little insight into the scope of practice or capabilities of others who work on their teams. In a large study conducted with staff providing team-based care in the Department of Veterans Affairs, researchers found that team members didn't understand the role of others, often underutilizing them, which led to significant challenges in effective care delivery.[11.]

The first step to promoting a team-based approach to care may involve changing the current perceptions of those working on teams about care delivery, the scope of practice of other disciplines, and the value of expertise brought by other team members. Role clarity is essential. Every team member must clearly understand other members' unique contributions, educational backgrounds, areas of high achievement, and limitations. A common issue in team-based care is the problem of "turf battles." These turf battles may involve struggles over protecting the scope and authority of a profession.

Team members may be reluctant to take advice or suggestions from other team members. A recent study examining the relationship between

RNs and CNAs on teams found that while the RNs believed they had positive relationships with the nursing assistants, the CNAs saw things differently. They thought that RNs did not use them to their full potential in the role and did not recognize their role stressors.[12]

To work effectively, each member must have confidence that other team members can meet their responsibilities. There may be concerns of legal liability for one's practice or losing control over a one-to-one relationship with patients. Kiara observed this problem when LPNs were integrated into her acute care unit nursing teams. Although paired to deliver care to nine patients collaboratively, the RNs complained that they were jeopardizing their licenses by assigning care to their LPN partners even when it was within their scope of practice. Most RNs in her unit had only worked in primary nursing care models, so working on teams was new to them, as were the principles of assignment delegation discussed in Chapter 4.

Kiara designed a graphic for her unit (Figure 12) that clearly outlined the responsibilities of each team member. She posted it on the unit and reviewed it multiple times in shift huddles. Her health system in Massachusetts has a broader scope of practice for LPNs than in some other states. Before developing the graphic, she ensured the assignments accurately reflected the state's scope of practice and her health system's position descriptions.

FIGURE 12

LPN and RN Assignments

LPN Assignments	RN Assignments
Routine Charting of Assigned Tasks and Focused Patient Assessments	New Admission, Discharge Assessments and Change in Condition Assessment
Implement Physician Orders Once Reviewed if in Scope	Acknowledgement of Orders in Record or Taking Verbal Orders
Reinforcement of Patient Teaching	Planning of Patient Education about Medications and Diagnosis
Administration of Medications and Insulin, Vaccinations within Scope	Administration of High-Risk Medications, IV Medications or Titration of Medications
Tracheostomy Care and Suctioning	Removal of Patients from Oxygen if D/C
Vital Signs	Decisions about Contacting a Physician about a Change in Patient Status
Place, Monitor, and Remove Peripheral IVs and Midline Catheters, Draw Blood	Accepting Calls or Texts on Critical Lab Values

Getting role clarity right is an essential part of team-based care. Roles and responsibilities can change over time when adding new team members or revising position descriptions.

A TEAM-FIRST MINDSET

Throughout his decades-long nursing career, Darnell had never thought much about teamwork. It seemed like such a natural part of nursing. During the past couple of years, he has seen a change in how many younger nurses view teamwork and collaboration. Darnell has some nurses who have no interest in being team players. He told one nurse that she seemed more concerned with her assignment in a vacuum regardless of what was happening with the rest of the team. She unapologetically agreed that this was true. He observed that everything seemed to be me, me, and more me for this nurse. When he mentioned the importance of teamwork, some of his staff told him they were there to put in their 12 hours and do their jobs, not focus on what others were doing.

Darnell's concerns are shared by many leaders today. Our youngest generation of nurses, Generation Z (born between 1997 and 2021), see teamwork differently than previous generational cohorts. We know from generational research that we develop attitudes, values, and beliefs based on collective experiences. In a report from the Walton Family Foundation, researchers found that what makes this generation of Americans unique is that Generation Z has come of age in a time of tremendous national chaos and trauma. Unlike other generations, Generation Z has not seen a united country. Generation Z is also the only generation to grow up entirely in the digital age. For better or worse, social media is not just a tool; it's a part of their identity. Social influencers on these platforms emphasize caring for your career and financial well-being because no one else will. Individual needs are prioritized over the needs of the group.[13]

Against this backdrop, leaders like Darnell are trying to promote teamwork and a team-first mindset as a value. Generation Z is more self-directed and independent than previous generations but often lacks real-world wisdom and experience they could gain from closer observation of others on the team.[14] Seeing value in what the team can accomplish versus any individual is essential. Darnell recognized that a team-first mindset needed to begin with how he coaches the staff as their leader. To build a team-first perspective, he began to do the following:

- Talk about the "team" rather than using the word staff.
- Promote team backup by placing backup buddies on team assignments.
- Correct staff who talk about "my" patients versus "our" patients
- Recognize the achievement of the team versus individual recognition whenever possible.

- Ask individuals who come to him with requests how the request would impact the team.
- Value and call out the diversity of strengths of the team.
- Refer staff to other team members who could help in problem-solving.
- Include teamwork as an essential competency in his evaluations.
- Question staff applying for positions about their teamwork experiences.
- Ask patients about teamwork among those giving care during leader rounding.

Darnell wisely realizes that establishing a solid team foundation involves a shared mindset and attitude that promotes collaboration, cooperation, and mutual support. A change to a team-first perspective would not happen overnight on his team, but taking small incremental steps in how he led the team would bring them closer to the goal.

KEY POINTS

✓ Before teams can work together effectively, there must be a foundation to help promote teamwork.

✓ Psychological safety and trust matter more to team outcomes than individual expertise.

✓ Shared values give team members reasons for caring about what they do, making a difference in work attitudes and performance.

✓ Every team member must clearly understand other members' unique contributions, educational backgrounds, areas of high achievement, and limitations.

✓ Our youngest generation of nurses, Generation Z (born between 1997 and 2021), see teamwork differently than previous generational cohorts.

CHAPTER 7

ASSESSING TEAM FUNCTIONING

Sometimes leaders are reluctant to evaluate sensitive topics in team cultures like trust, psychological safety, and communication. They may feel they already know the problems or fear difficult feedback. But you need baseline data as a team to learn and grow. If you don't ask, you won't know what to start doing, stop doing, or continue doing to build a culture of teamwork. Oki is a perioperative director in a large academic medical center. Until the COVID pandemic, she had a cohesive team with many seasoned staff members. Unfortunately, most of Oki's experienced nurses retired during the pandemic. Today, her team comprises new graduates and nurses on travel contracts. She sees the changes in the team culture and wants to work to rebuild it.

When assessing the culture of her team, Oki could do a Strengths, Weaknesses, Opportunities, and Threats (SWOT) Analysis (Part 4 Toolkit) and involve her team in determining how well they currently work together. The SWOT analysis will help Oki look at the team's strengths and areas of vulnerability. Team members might view the team culture differently depending on their roles and working schedules. There are often subcultures within cultures on teams, so Oki needs to get broad input on team functioning. Once she has these results, she can develop plans to rebuild the team culture, focusing on critical areas of concern such as:

- Team communication
- Team trust
- Team conflict
- Team accountability
- Team connectedness
- Team engagement
- Team well-being

TEAM DYSFUNCTION

Oki's story is not unusual. With the recent turbulence in the healthcare environment and staff turnover, many teams today lack the strong cultures they once had. Teams can slowly drift into dysfunction by default. Patrick Lencioni describes the following five signs of dysfunctional teams:[3]

1. **An Absence of Trust** – occurs because of an inability to show vulnerability about what you know and what you don't. When there is trust in teams, political gamesmanship is reduced. Lencioni contends that a lack of trust often happens because team members know little about one another's personal stories.
2. **A Fear of Conflict** – effective teams must learn to manage inevitable conflict. When teams navigate conflict effectively, they can move past differences and avoid making the conflict destructive. Lencioni writes that teams must be OK with constructive debate

to manage conflict effectively. Navigating conflict in teams is discussed in Chapter 9.

3. **A Lack of Commitment** – high-performing teams recognize that individual opinions will not always win out and that everyone needs to commit to implementation once a decision is made. Lencioni contends that sometimes it is impossible to reach a team consensus, and sometimes team members must agree to disagree.

4. **An Avoidance of Accountability** – effective teams hold one another accountable. They provide backup to other team members and do what they say they will do.

5. **An Inattention to Results** – effective teams are results-focused and worry about the impact of their work on quality and safe patient care.

Gallup researchers have found that definitions of team culture — "how we do things around here" — have changed tremendously in recent years.[15] Cultural drift is the gradual, uncontrolled changing of a team culture over time, with its distinctive norms, values, and behavior patterns. Culture develops either by design or by default. Lapses in teamwork, loyalty, and professional accountability can happen gradually in cultures if values are not reinforced. You can see a normalization of team behaviors emerge that are incongruent with a culture of quality, safety, and inclusion.

Oki's team, before the pandemic, was cohesive and had worked together for an extended time. In a SWOT analysis, she may find that the level of trust among team members is low or that the team cannot deal effectively with conflict. With so many travel nurses in her perioperative area, she must closely examine team members' accountability levels and set expectations if they are not being met. Teams can quickly become dysfunctional when members work in silos and are not situationally attentive to what is happening with the group.

Situational Awareness

Teams perform more effectively when their members are alert and aware of what is happening with other team members.[16] When situationally aware, teams can provide backup support, make assignment adjustments, and more effectively manage team emotions. Situational awareness is essential in clinical areas like emergency departments, where conditions can change rapidly.

Lorenzo manages a busy emergency department (ED) and recently hired many new graduates. He noticed that some of his new staff were sitting down and texting on their phones when their team members were involved in crises and needed help. They seemed oblivious to what was happening in their environment. When he questioned the team members about why they were not helping others, they told him they had finished their work and did not know anyone needed help. Lorenzo realized that he would have to be more intentional about teaching situational awareness to his team. He discussed it during a team meeting and posted signs throughout the ED reminding staff, "*None of us sits down until all of us can sit down.*"

Teams with high situational awareness pay attention to the following areas:

1. How are others on the team doing?
2. Does anyone need my help to catch up with their assignment?
3. How cohesive are we as a team?
4. Where are we struggling as a team?
5. What is happening in the environment that could impact the team?
6. Is our workload increasing?
7. What shifts do we need to make in our assignments?

Lorenzo realizes that some team members are naturally situationally aware, but others need to be taught and are more inwardly focused.

He needed to be more explicit about what to keep an eye on in the environment.

Team Engagement

Engagement and satisfaction surveys indicate that many staff in health-care don't feel involved in the decision-making process. The flip side is that getting team members to attend or be involved in professional governance is complicated. Many nurses tell their leaders they don't have the emotional bandwidth to do anything but come to work, put in their 12 hours, and go home. Nadia is a clinical leader on a team with Gallup engagement scores that indicate that a significant percentage of her team is either disengaged or actively disengaged in their work.

Nadia is not alone in struggling with team engagement. After trending up in recent years, employee engagement in the US is steadily declining - dropping from 36% engaged employees in 2020 to 32% in 2022. The most significant decline was in healthcare; now, only 29% of staff report feeling engaged.[17] Gallup also found a six-point decrease in the percentage of employees who are extremely satisfied with their organization as a good workplace. These all indicate that employees feel more disconnected from their employers and teams.

One notable concern is the drop in nurse participation in shared gov-ernance structures. Nadia's hospital is Magnet ® designated, so involvement in the unit practice council activities is highly encouraged and required for clinical ladder advancement. When Nadia asked the team about getting more involved, they finally said, *"Can't you find some more straightforward way to involve us that does not include coming in on our days off."* They also wondered about the effectiveness of shared decision-making because the same agenda items appeared month after month with no closure in the decision loop.

Nadia decided to take a different approach in involving her team in decision-making. Their practice council meetings are now on the Zoom platform. The meeting agendas usually have no more than three items and a 12-minute timeslot for each agenda item. Nadia urges her team to attend when a decision is on the schedule that is important to them. The meetings are kept to 45 minutes and are recorded and posted to their unit's Facebook® page. She adds fun to the discussion by awarding prizes at each meeting. Staff can be on-camera or off-camera. They come off mute to voice opinions or put their comments in the chat. Nadia uses the polling function for decisions and ideas. The meeting starts with closing the loop on decisions from previous sessions. Younger staff come in from home on their phones – some are on treadmills. She even has nurses who attend part of the meeting on their phones while on a break from work. Nadia is trying to meet the team where they are and asks them, "How can we do this better?"

Nadia is right to be concerned about nurse disengagement on her team. A strong predictor of team performance is team members' engagement levels. Vicki Hess is an employee engagement expert. She developed an engagement formula: *Satisfied + Energized + Productive at Work = Employee Engagement*. *Satisfied* is when you are psychologically connected with the work. *Energized* means you are willing to put effort into your work. *Productive* means that our efforts contribute to the organization's overall vision and bottom line, and it is verifiable.[18] Nurse engagement is sometimes described as nurses' commitment to and satisfaction with their jobs, but it involves more than that. Nurses commit themselves to their team, the organization, and the nursing profession when engaged. The team culture will be more positive with higher levels of engagement.

Managing Team Negativity

During the past three years, healthcare teams have experienced high turnover and disruptive change. We now find ourselves in a place where we lack many things, especially staff. It has led to more anger, disillusionment, and chronic complaining than leaders have ever contended with before. There are no easy fixes to any of what is happening, but it is becoming clear that constant complaining may worsen the situation. Dexter, a new leader, is struggling with negativity on his team. He works hard to keep a positive attitude and avoid the corrosiveness that negativity can bring to groups. His strategies have included the following:

- He does not feed into the negativity himself.
- He has coached some negative staff using the situation-behavior-impact approach described in Chapter 5.
- He keeps team discussions about things within the team's circle of influence and out of their circle of concern (Part 4 – Toolkit).
- He communicates the progress that the team is making despite the current challenges.
- He stays future-focused and solutions-oriented.

Despite all these efforts, team negativity is still a problem for Dexter. He decides to try a different approach. He is using the work of Will Bowen to build a complaint-free team culture.[19] Bowen has developed his work from a Maya Angelou quote – *"If you don't like something, change it. If you can't change it – change your attitude."*

Bowen has researched the complaining behavior and contends that it can quickly become habitual. Most of us are inclined to have a negative bias about things. These feelings can easily exacerbate when surrounded by negative team members whose conversations evolve into chronic complaining. While this may feel good, research demonstrates that when we complain less, we are happier. Our overall well-being is better. When we complain, we focus on what is wrong and do not move toward improvement. In a sense, we disempower ourselves. New staff quickly pick up on a culture of complaint when it has become normalized. It is not a recipe for retention on teams.

Bowen developed a program designed to build a complaint-free environment. He does not suggest that all complaining is unjustified;

instead, it is habitual for some. The goal is to shift the emotional compass of the environment from negative to positive. What people learn when they start a program is that they complain a lot more than they would like to believe. Criticism and sarcasm are both forms of complaining. In talking with his team members, Dexter finds that many staff feels like he does and that the negativity has made teamwork more challenging.

Bowen recommends a 21-day challenge to a complaint-free environment. More than 15 million people worldwide have taken up the challenge of going twenty-one consecutive days without complaining, criticizing, or gossiping. In doing so, you form new positive habits. You wear a wrist bracelet as a potent reminder. Bowen suggests switching the bracelet from wrist to wrist with each spoken complaint until you go 21 consecutive days without complaining. He warns that if you complain a lot, this may take far longer than 21 days. The goal is to change your thoughts by changing your words and then beginning to create a better culture by design. Dexter buys everyone on the team bracelets and has set up a reward system for those who go 21 days without complaining. Dexter is not guaranteed to turn around a team culture using this strategy, but he is confident it will decrease the negativity.

Teams at Night

Healthcare is unusual in that much of the work is 24/7. Two or more teams may care for patients within 24 hours. Managers often struggle with conflicts between their day and night shift staff. These problems have intensified in the current environment as fewer full-time staff want to work a night shift, and staff on travel contracts or new graduates often fill roles on nights. These changes can leave your night tour staff feeling unsupported, isolated, and disengaged. Left unchecked, you may find two very different cultures on the same unit and potential differences in practice. At worst, it can lead to conflict between shifts that destroys unit morale and causes team dysfunction. The nurse manager on the unit plays an integral role in how teams across shifts work together.

Here are some dos and don'ts to consider in your assessment and leadership of the night shift: [20-21]

DO

1. Keep in regular contact with the administrative supervisors who work nights to obtain their perspective on the functioning of your unit on that tour. Ask them to contact you if they see problems you should know about immediately.
2. Schedule yourself to work all or part of the night shift quarterly. Let the staff know you will be working and are there to listen to their concerns.
3. Establish some protocols for what type of situations you want to be immediately notified about but avoid taking too many calls or texts at night.
4. Demonstrate gratitude for the team who work the night tour and recognize the inconvenience and sacrifices they make in their personal lives.
5. Arrange regular huddles with your night tour staff to communicate policy and practice changes or establish a unit Facebook® page.
6. Consider using a web platform to stream your staff meeting so your night shift can participate.
7. Maintain ongoing contact with the night shift team leaders for their input into unit decisions.
8. Support your staff in their communication with physicians at night.
9. Be proactive in managing any conflict that you observe between the shifts.

10. Encourage healthy well-being and advocate for the night shift to have access to cafeteria food and other amenities.

DON'T

1. Assume that the workload on nights is lighter than on dayshift.
2. Ignore signs of extreme staff fatigue or sleep deprivation and whether it is safe for a staff member to drive home.
3. Question a decision at night without hearing the whole story and considering the available resources.
4. Change policies or practices on the unit without input from the night tour.
5. Lower your hiring standards because you are desperate to fill night shift positions.
6. Let conflict fester between the day and night shifts without intervention.
7. Destroy your personal life by responding to regular texts at night or coming in early every day to meet with the night shift and then staying late.
8. Tolerate a higher level of absenteeism on the night shift.
9. Forget to include your night shift staff in disaster and crisis training.
10. Allow night staff to opt out of self-governance initiatives.

On most 24/7 units, between 30% and 40% of your staff will work the night tour. Without active collaboration with their manager, these team members can quickly feel they work in a different hospital than the day tour. Night shift teams play a unique role in units in keeping patients safe while the rest of the staff sleeps. They need to feel valued and respected for the work that they do.

Key Points

✓ A SWOT analysis of team functioning will provide essential data to improve a team's culture.

✓ If you don't ask, you won't know what to start doing, stop doing, or continue doing to build a culture of teamwork.

✓ Cultural drift is the gradual, uncontrolled changing of a team culture over time, with its distinctive norms, values, and behavior patterns.

✓ New staff quickly pick up on a culture of complaining when it has become normalized.

✓ Without active collaboration with their manager, night team members can quickly feel they work in a different hospital than the day tour.

CHAPTER 8

MANAGING TEAM COMMUNICATION

I had a mentor who often said that the "soft skills" are often the "hard skills" to master. Communication is undoubtedly at the top of that hard skills list. Poor communication skills in healthcare environments can lead to medical errors, fragmented care, poor team coordination, and incivility. Most problems that occur in teams are traceable back to challenges with communication. Communication in healthcare environments is difficult in the best of times.

Today's teams are large and work together sporadically. When times become turbulent, transparent communication often does not happen. Too much communication about what the team is not doing will make it feel critical and create a hostile culture. In a recent study by Deloitte conducted for the American Organization of Nurse Leaders, frontline leaders report that more supportive and transparent communication on teams is critical to team success.[22]

By 2030, three-quarters of the healthcare workforce will be either Millennials or Generation Z. Email is not their preferred method of communication. Yet, it is the official channel in most organizations.[23] Younger staff who grew up with cell phones and texting may have challenges communicating face-to-face with their colleagues, patients, and families. Problems often center around talking too much at the wrong times, interrupting colleagues and their leader, failing to respond to administrative emails, poor conduct in team meetings, and sending inappropriate comments in text messages and emails.

Team leaders are often surprised at how often they must communicate the same message. Mateo found this when he transitioned from a charge nurse role to a clinical leader of a team. He worked hard to give staff consistent messages in huddles and text important information. Yet still, many on his team reported that they had not heard about a new policy change. Mateo was frustrated but began to realize that messages are rarely received and completely understood the first time they are shared. It is not a one-and-done activity. He now jokingly tells his team – "No, I don't have dementia, and yes, I have said this many times before."

Marketing experts recommend using *the rule of 7* based on research that it can take up to seven times for an audience to act on the message.[24] You should also plan to use three or more channels to communicate important information. These channels include team huddles, communication boards, newsletters, group text messages, emails, a unit Facebook page, or a staff meeting. Storytelling is powerful in leadership. If you present changes in policies or practices, stories are an excellent way to convey the why behind messages and reconnect staff to their purpose. As he looked at communication on his team, Mateo realized that frequently communicating messages was not enough; the quality of his communication was also critical. He had been in the military and found that the BLUF communication format (Bottom Line Up Front) was also helpful with his team in focusing them on the most crucial part of administrative messages.

TEACHING TEAMS EFFECTIVE COMMUNICATION

Teaching team members to communicate effectively with one another can be challenging. Although our focus is usually on verbal communication skills, team members also communicate with each other in the following four different ways:

Verbal – the words that you use and how you structure your messages. Verbal communication is the most critical point of interaction between team members. Whether your team talks face to face, over the phone, or through video conferencing, these conversations can decide how one person perceives the other.

Nonverbal – your body language, including gestures, facial expressions, and eye contact. Many people aren't aware of how nonverbal communication affects their relationships. More than half of all communication is nonverbal, so paying attention to nonverbal cues is essential. Nonverbal cues are more challenging in acute healthcare environments where mask-wearing is still the norm.

Para-Verbal – the tone, pacing, and pitch of your voice. There are regional differences in how communication is paced. Team members from different parts of the country may be viewed as communicating too rapidly or too slowly. Some team members have naturally loud voices that might be perceived as aggressive, others may speak softly, and team members may have challenges hearing what is being said.

Digital Presence – digital communication via email, texts, and social media. Team members need guidance about using digital communication and when to communicate digitally versus using other communication channels.

Bruce Tulgan, a generational expert, suggests that team leaders must establish clear communication standards within the workgroup and on the unit. Some best practices he recommends in coaching staff include the following:[25]

- Advise team members to listen twice as much as they talk.
- Urge team members not to interrupt each other or check their phones while others speak to them.
- Respect the viewpoints of others even if you disagree.
- Take responsibility for the power of your words.
- Exhibit respect, courtesy, and kindness when in conversations with others.
- Communicate as concisely as possible using the BLUF format described above.
- Value excellent communication as an essential skill to advance one's career.

Evidence-Based Communication Strategies

The complex tasks involved in most healthcare procedures can introduce communication risks, such as role confusion within the team, interruptions, noise, and incomplete handoffs. Most quality and safety issues on healthcare teams occur because of communication problems. Clear communication is critical but not always easy to achieve. Fortunately, good tools are available to help communicate more effectively and, even more critically, ensure that communication is understood.

Strategies and Tools to Enhance Performance and Patient Safety (TeamSTEPPS®) is an evidence-based communication model developed for clinical practice with funding from the Agency for Healthcare Research and Quality.[26] These tools were developed for team members to communicate effectively and build safer patient care environments.

Tools in the model include SBAR, the Two-Challenge Rule, Call-Outs, and Check-Backs.

SBAR - was designed to communicate critical information requiring immediate attention and action concerning a patient's condition. It is also widely used as part of patient handoffs. **Situation**—What is going on with the patient? **Background**—What is the clinical background or context? **Assessment**—What do I think the problem is? **Recommendation and Request**—What would I do to correct it?

The Two-Challenge Rule - requires the communicator to voice their concern at least twice to receive an acknowledgment from the receiver. This rule is invoked when a healthcare team member suggests or performs an intervention that deviates from the standard of care. The nurse would assertively voice their concern at least two times. If the challenged team member does not acknowledge this concern, the leader would take more decisive action or utilize the hospital chain of command as needed.

Call-Outs –is a strategy that leaders can use to inform all team members of crucial information during emergencies to help team members be situationally aware and anticipate what comes next.

Check-Back requires the sender of the communication to verify the information the other team member received or use closed-loop communication. Close-loop communication is associated with higher team effectiveness.

END-OF-SHIFT REPORTS

With so much team turnover, many hospitals have implemented checklists to guide team communication, such as change of shift reports. If teams fail to share important information, team effectiveness suffers. In healthcare, patient handoffs from one team member to another are often problematic, resulting in patient safety issues. Claire's team on a medical-surgical unit is comprised primarily of new graduates. Most had little experience in their nursing programs, giving or receiving the change of shift report on their assigned patients. She needed to establish ground rules for communication to avoid misunderstandings. Her unit had tried report templates, but none were effective. Claire researched the problem and found AHQR-recommended guidelines.[27] She developed a report template for her team to improve communication. The AHQR guidelines outline the following key areas to include in the bedside shift report checklist:

- A formal introduction of nursing staff to patients and family members.
- Inclusion of the patient and family in the discussion.
- Verbal report using the SBAR format described above.
- A focused assessment of the patient, equipment in the room, and any safety hazards.
- A review of tasks to be done on the shift, such as lab work, medication administration, and patient teaching.
- Discussion about discharge planning.
- Patient and family concerns and goals.

Claire found that hardwiring how end-of-shift communication occurred on the team improved the quality of the reports and the confidence of the staff.

Sharpening Team Listening Skills

Once Claire developed the end-of-shift report, she realized that there was another step in the process. Her team members needed to become better listeners. The medical-surgical unit was busy, and team members were often easily distracted. When discussing team communication, we often forget the importance of listening. To achieve effective teamwork, members must carefully listen to one another respectfully and ask thoughtful questions.

Listening is a skill that you can learn. Not listening is a habit and one you can break. Claire has several nurses on her team who become impatient during team reports, often breaking into conversations instead of letting others finish their thoughts. She had arm bands made for the team with the word WAIT imprinted. It is an acronym for **W**hy **A**m I **T**alking? *The armbands are a reminder to* quiet your agenda. The most effective team members leave others with the feeling of being heard.

When team members do not listen to each other, it can lead to anger, disappointment, and disrespect. A failure to listen in teams can ultimately lead to serious communication breakdowns and medical errors. When everyone listens, the team feels more engaged, valued, respected, and hopeful. Authentic dialogue does not happen when we pretend to listen and will not happen if we do not listen at all.

A TEAM CULTURE OF PROFESSIONAL FEEDBACK

To ensure quality in communication, team members must feel they can safely provide each other with feedback. Team members sometimes avoid sharing input because of a cognitive bias known as "everyone already knows." We assume everyone else on the team also knows because we know or observe something. The risk of this is especially prevalent in teaming environments where new team members don't receive feedback and may not have information known by long-timers. In high turnover environments, the shelf life of shared understanding about things shortens, making feedback crucially important.[16]

Kevin is a clinical leader on a team with professional feedback challenges. Some on his team are perfectionists who view any constructive feedback as indicating failure. Others become very defensive and lash out at the person giving feedback. New graduates complain about their preceptors being bullies and give themselves high ratings on their competency assessments. Psychologists have a term for what Kevin was experiencing. It is called the Dunning-Krueger effect. This concept comes from a solid body of research that people who are the least competent in a field often rate their performance higher than it is because they don't yet appreciate the nuances of expert practice. It is not surprising that we see more of this today. Most acute care units have high percentages of less seasoned nurses. Many young nurses don't experience that awe when they watch a mentor intuitively grasp that the patient is crashing, even before any data exists.

Kevin knows he needs a team culture mindset change about professional feedback. All of us continually need feedback about our performance in the following three key areas:

1. **Continue doing** – things as a team member that contribute to excellent patient care, teamwork, or professional growth.
2. **Stop doing** – things don't meet expected standards of care, teamwork, or professional growth and could derail us if we don't change.
3. **Start doing** – things to grow in our practice, build skills in working with others or raise our game in developing ourselves as professionals.

When interviewing new nurses, I recommend that you let them know they will receive professional feedback and why feedback is vital in their careers. Feedback should always be framed as giving an evaluation of the work and not about the person. If a team member later resists feedback, remind them you discussed this during their interview. As a leader, you must also be open to feedback about your performance. Leaders should serve as role models. Make it safe to give and receive feedback. Nurses can't be fully professionally socialized into their roles without feedback. We owe it to our younger staff to help them learn and grow, even if they initially resist. You don't want them to derail in their careers but rather become their best possible self.

Key Points

✓ Most problems that occur in teams are related to challenges with communication.

✓ Strategies and Tools to Enhance Performance and Patient Safety (TeamSTEPPS®) is an evidence-based communication model developed for clinical practice with funding from the Agency for Healthcare Research and Quality

✓ Patient handoffs from one team member are often problematic to another resulting in patient safety issues.

✓ To achieve effective teamwork, members must carefully listen to one another respectfully and ask thoughtful questions.

✓ Team members must be able to provide each other with feedback to achieve high-quality outcomes.

CHAPTER 9

NAVIGATING CONFLICT ON TEAMS

Today's healthcare workforce includes staff with different values, beliefs, and attitudes. These differences can and do lead to conflict. Couple this with a society that has become increasingly divisive. Unsurprisingly, frontline nurse leaders report that managing team conflict requires increasing time and provides little satisfaction in their work.[22] Helping teams move past their differences and effectively work together is challenging yet necessary.

Patrick Lencioni, known for his work on team dysfunction, has written about the importance of trust and conflict acceptance in healthy team cultures. His research indicates that a team's inability to resolve conflict successfully is one of the five characteristics of dysfunctional teams.[3] Nowhere are the stakes higher than health care, where team synergy and interdependence are necessary for high-quality patient outcomes. Conflict is central to all interactions because of the diversity of human experience. But in leadership, it can also be very time-consuming.

Angela was surprised at how much conflict there was in her NICU unit. She recently became an assistant manager with responsibility for scheduling. Nurses on her team asked not to be scheduled with other staff because of interpersonal conflicts. They even warned her they might call in if their requests were not accommodated. Angela saw herself as easygoing and able to get along with just about anyone. She hated conflict and tried to avoid it whenever possible. She had even thought about making the unit a no-conflict zone. Some leaders like Angela see conflict as undesirable and fail to recognize that it can provide a source of growth and creativity. When your staff successfully manages conflict, it can lead to better decision-making, process improvements, and team cohesiveness. In her new role, avoiding conflict would not be possible. She needed to change her mindset about the usefulness of conflict to help her team (Figure 13).

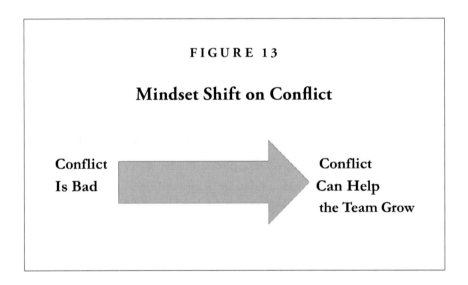

FIGURE 13

Mindset Shift on Conflict

Conflict
Is Bad

Conflict
Can Help
the Team Grow

Angela talked with the NICU team about staffing and scheduling. She would not allow the interpersonal conflicts that staff have with one another to drive scheduling. Angela would be happy to work with the team to mediate their disputes. While it was not her expectation that all the staff would have friendships with one another, she did expect respectful, collegial working relationships. Angela knew that to be effective; she needed to develop competency in managing conflict. Her former mindset was that conflict is destructive. Shifting her mindset to believe that navigating conflict can lead to growth is vital. Self-awareness about your attitudes toward conflict is essential.

TEAM STYLES OF MANAGING CONFLICT

Not every team member manages conflict in the same way, nor should every conflict be handled using only one conflict management style. Although many of us can flex our style when needed, we usually have a preferred method of managing conflict, which is essential to identify. The most widely used assessment uses the styles outlined in the Thomas Kilmann Conflict Resolution Model.[28] There are five primary modes of managing conflict, depending on assertiveness versus cooperativeness. These five styles include the following: avoiding, accommodating, competing, collaborating, and compromising.

- **Competing** is an assertive and uncooperative approach to conflict. Team members using this style pursue their concerns with little regard for the other's interests. It is a power-oriented approach to a conflict where you defend your position and follow what you believe to be your rights. Your goal in conflict situations is to win.

- **Accommodating** is an unassertive and cooperative approach to managing conflict, which is the opposite of competing. Team members who use this style ignore their needs to satisfy the other party's concerns. These team members seek harmony in their relationships with others regardless of personal costs.

- **Avoiding** is both an unassertive and uncooperative response to conflict. Team members who avoid conflict might intentionally overlook a contentious issue, postpone a discussion, or withdraw entirely from the conflict situation.

- **Collaborating** is an assertive and cooperative response that is the opposite of avoiding. Team members who use this style of managing conflict work with others to find a solution that fully satisfies others' needs and concerns while meeting their own needs.

- **Compromising** is an approach where you moderate your level of assertiveness and cooperativeness. Team members who use this style seek a mutually acceptable win-win solution for both individuals.

Erika is a perioperative director. Her OR team constantly complains about working with a group of surgeons who are in it to win it using a competitive style whenever there are points of disagreement. Erika has her team take a conflict management style assessment and finds most of her nurses have a default style of either avoiding conflict or accommodating the needs of others. She explains to the team that it is essential to be able to flex your default style depending on the nature of the conflict.

A current conflict with one of the surgeons provides an excellent example of a conflict that the team needs to address. According to their protocol, the OR team must conduct a "time-out" before the start of any surgical procedure. During the time-out, the entire operating room team reviews the patient's identity, the procedure, and the site before the surgical incision or the start of the procedure. An eye surgeon who does procedures that typically last 15 minutes feels that time-outs on short surgeries are a waste of time and refuses to participate. Team members cannot avoid this conflict and must collaborate with the surgeon in order to follow hospital protocol.

We should develop the capability to use all five modes of conflict resolution depending on the type of conflict. Awareness about your preferred style is critical because it could be your default style, particularly in stressful situations. Studies indicate that many nurse leaders use avoidance as their primary response to conflict.[29] Nurse leaders whose preferred natural style is avoidance will need to push themselves to engage in conflict resolution, especially when it is contentious. In contrast, if a nurse leader is naturally overly competitive in style, they may have challenges reaching successful conflict resolution because their approach is too combative. The key is identifying the right approach for each unique situation and then flexing your default style.

Getting to the Root of Team Conflicts

There are two major types of conflict. Functional conflict, called cognitive conflict, is disagreement about roles, tasks, issues, ideas, principles, or processes. The second type of conflict is relationship conflict. These conflicts involve people or their values and often focus on who is right.[30] Relationship conflicts can quickly escalate into attacks, blaming, and verbal microaggressions.

Experts contend that there are always antecedents to any team conflict situation. Before a leader intervenes in a team conflict, they must assess why it occurred. The antecedent conditions are what started the conflict. An example of this could be that the charge nurse changes the assignment of staff nurses during the shift because of issues with patient throughput. The staff nurse and charge nurse might get into a conflict even when there are valid reasons for a change in assignment. In most situations, diagnosing systems or personal issues that led to a conflict is essential.

Sometimes, team members have relationships outside the work setting that deteriorate and cause work conflicts. Differences in generational values, beliefs, and attitudes can cause team conflict. Generation Z nurses are more likely to discuss mental health and well-being at work. This level of openness about emotions may aggravate team members of older generations who feel they should leave their challenges at home and not discuss them at work. Many teams now have travel nurses who work as part of core staffing. Some travelers readily talk about their salary versus the full-time staff. Resentment in teams can quickly build and lead to staff conflicts.

Many nurse leaders have told me that the polarization of society has seeped into the work environment. It has led to negativity, conflict, and incivility. Creating work environments that embrace the diversity of thought is now considered a new frontier in leadership. Research by Deloitte and other consulting groups indicates that the highest-performing teams are both cognitively and demographically diverse.[31] Acceptance of diversity of ideas and viewpoints does not happen in environments unless inclusion is promoted as a core value.

I interviewed a nurse leader to learn how she manages the diversity of viewpoints among staff. She talks with her team frequently about the importance of accepting that everyone is entitled to their perspective. You don't have to agree with the viewpoint, but you should be willing to listen. She tries to role-model this behavior herself. When she heard two staff loudly arguing about politics, she dropped into the conversation and asked – "Spend five minutes here and try to come to a consensus on two things you can agree on." She understands the social drivers of human behavior and that bringing staff to common ground is the first step.

MEDITATING CONFLICT SITUATIONS

Not every conflict needs leadership intervention, yet some escalate quickly if no action is taken. Team leaders have three choices in conflict situations.

The first is to do nothing. Doing nothing could be the right choice if you anticipate that the conflict will quickly resolve or is time limited. If a dispute is between two team members, and one has already accepted a position in another unit, the leader may decide not to get involved. The second choice is to coach team members to mediate their conflict. Sometimes, disputes can be settled by staff members without the leader intervening. Not intervening can be the right choice if individuals have a good working relationship. It will also be a good decision if the situation involves a charge nurse who needs to develop conflict resolution skills in their role. A third choice is to become directly involved and mediate the dispute.

Ideally, you want to coach your team members to work through conflict, but sometimes this is impossible. Look for the following warning signs that indicate it is time to get involved:

1. The staff members are not respectful to one another.
2. A staff member has threatened to resign because of the conflict.
3. The conflict is impacting team morale or quality of care.

Isabel, a behavioral health team leader, decided to mediate a conflict. Two team members had a long-standing dispute before she assumed her leadership role. Whenever they worked together on a shift, there was drama. They argued openly about assignments and refused to provide each other with the team backup needed for care. Before mediating the conflict, she sought to learn as much as possible about why it was happening. The two staff members were from different generational groups and had different beliefs. One believed the other lacked a good work ethic. What began as minor disagreements had escalated over time. They lost respect for one another. Isabel knew this conflict mediation would be challenging and recognized that it impacted care and morale. She planned the session using the following conflict resolution process recommended by experts: [32]

1. Bring the individuals in conflict together to discuss the problem. Although you may encounter resistance, bring the individuals together. As a leader, you want to create psychological safety for those involved in the dispute. If you allow each side to tell their story without others involved in the conflict present, you risk polarizing their positions and eroding trust. Conflict resolution conversations should not be one-sided monologues.

2. Agree to ground rules for discussion acceptable to all parties. When mediating a conflict, it is important to establish ground rules about behavior and language expected during the debate. These ground rules could include no interruption, no personal attacks, the word "I" to specify personal reactions, and no discussion of issues unrelated to this conflict.

3. Let each person clarify their perspective and opinion on the issues. Those involved in the conflict should share their views and what outcomes they hope to achieve from the mediation. Open-ended questions to clarify feelings are essential. If a staff member feels disrespected, seek more information by asking what leads them to that conclusion. Applying a time limit to the discussion may be helpful. Doing so helps each person speak about the issues and reduces conversational clutter with little bearing on the conflict. The goal is to shift from blaming to clarifying one's needs in the dispute.

4. Highlight common ground. Finding common ground in conflict is significant because it can serve as a reference point to help bring the discussion back on track. Most staff will agree with a mutual goal to provide the best possible patient care. When conflict escalates, you can get the individuals back to the point of common ground.

5. Develop interventions collaboratively and agree to disagree on points of contention. Presenting a conflict as either a black-or-white or right-or-wrong situation heightens the tension. Work to help individuals develop interventions collaboratively. The conversation should be solutions-focused versus dwelling on the problems. Where there is a point of significant contention, it may be necessary to agree to disagree.

6. Summarize and identify the next steps. The final step is to summarize what was said, identify the next steps, and any follow-up discussions you may need to schedule. A positive outcome in most conflicts will be to open the lines of communication and re-establish working relationships. Leaders can help staff openly acknowledge the differences in attitudes, values, and beliefs that have led to the conflict and ways to be more respectful in the future.

Isabel carefully planned the mediation session with the two team members. She developed some questions to ask both staff members during the session:

What part have you played in this conflict?
How do you know your perspective is accurate?
Have you tried looking at this from your co-worker's perspective?
What needs to be true that is not true today to resolve this conflict?
What would a good outcome look like in this situation?
How will we know if the conflict is over?

Planning helped Isabel keep the conversation on track when emotions ran high. She set clear expectations that a failure to move toward more constructive conflict resolution was not an option. Isabel knew that this would not be a one-and-done conversation. She planned one, three, and six-week follow-up discussions to assess progress. She remained optimistic in her approach even though the talks were energy-draining.

Difficult Team Members

Some team members demonstrate challenging behaviors. They cause conflict and drama in even the most effective teams. Dr. Amy Gallo points out that certain colleagues act in ways they shouldn't and cause us to question ourselves. They create group conflict by excluding or rejecting others and threatening the sense of team belonging. We must make the space to choose a team response to difficult members that will result in growth, not conflict. Otherwise, they can do an amygdala hijack of the team, causing everyone to go into stressful fight-or-flight responses.

Gallo describes the following seven common archetypes of difficult team members:[33]

The Pessimist – these team members always have something negative to say even when things are going well. They complain about new initiatives, other team members, and their leaders but rarely offer constructive solutions.

The Victim – these team members feel sorry for themselves and often feel they do more work than anyone else on the team. They evade accountability by blaming others and pushing back on constructive criticism.

The Passive-Aggressive Team Member – these team members make promises they don't keep, ignore emails and other communication, shift blame to others and make snarky comments.

The Know-It-All – these team members display a "my way or the highway" approach to work. They position their ideas as superior and don't credit others for their contributions.

The Tormentor – these team members are bullies and mistreat others by giving them heavier assignments or micromanaging their work.

The Biased Team Member – these team members stereotype others, use derogatory words and demonstrate discriminatory behaviors.

The Political Operator – these team members brag about their success, take undue credit for their work, push their agendas, and seek to curry favor with those in power.

Susan is in a clinical leadership position working with a team of pediatric nurses. Several RN members have worked on the unit for years yet are very pessimistic. A nursing instructor talked with Susan because these nurses had questioned the students about why they wanted to be nurses. They also had negative things to say about their health system, urging the students to seek employment elsewhere. Their behaviors directly conflicted with their organization's plan to welcome and hopefully recruit students who rotated through their department. Susan wondered about their negativity since they chose to stay on the team and with their employer. She talked with them about being role models and asked what frustrations had led to these conversations with students. Susan acknowledged that nursing is hard but tried to reframe their perspective. Susan told them about the conflict this was causing with their academic partner, who was unsure whether this was a healthy clinical environment for students. Their pessimism was unhelpful, causing friction, and she needed to set new team norms.

Tips for Conflict Management with Difficult Team Members

Like Susan, many leaders need to manage conflict with difficult team members. You may be unsuccessful in changing their behavior or mediating the conflict, but you can control your response. Below are five strategies to use when in conflict with difficult people:[34]

1. **Focus on what you can control** – generally, you are experiencing well-established behavior patterns with difficult people. Nothing will change unless the team member takes accountability for their role in the conflict. You can point out the behavior, but it is not your responsibility to change it.

2. **Don't overreact** – the behaviors you witness from difficult people reflect where they are personally more than anything you may have said or done. When you see an explosive reaction in conflict situations, you can be sure that there are underlying emotions that the person is experiencing.

3. **Set ground rules** – remember that you teach other people how to treat you when in conflict. Let the team member know that you will respect them but expect to be treated with respect in return. Don't tolerate yelling; if necessary, tell the person that you need to remove yourself from the conflict.

4. **Use empathy** – you may disagree with their point of view but acknowledge that they appear very angry about the situation. It can be challenging to be stuck in a place of negativity or anger. Empathy can sometimes help to de-escalate explosive conflict situations.

5. **Talk less and listen more** – listening can be a powerful tool in team conflict. Less conversation is often more effective with difficult people. Use short, concise messages to drive your point home, and set a time limit on how much you will engage in the discussion. Avoid using the word "attitude" because this is subjective, but instead, focus on the behavior.

KEY POINTS

✓ When your staff successfully manages conflict, it can lead to better decision-making, process improvements, and team cohesiveness.

✓ If your paradigm is that conflict is destructive, you are less likely to engage in constructive conflict.

✓ Not every leader manages conflict in the same way, nor should every conflict be handled using only one conflict management style.

✓ Before a leader intervenes in a team conflict, they need to assess how it occurred accurately.

✓ Some team members are difficult. They cause conflict and drama in even the most effective working teams.

CHAPTER 10

FOCUSING ON QUALITY AND SAFETY

V
alue-based care is the driver of reimbursement in today's healthcare system. Excellent patient outcomes that are high value
occur in cultures with a relentless focus on safety and quality.
Team culture significantly impacts many metrics that are now key in
healthcare environments and drive payment. During the pandemic,
some quality and safety activities took a back seat in the face of rapidly
accelerating disease transmission trends with COVID. Unfortunately,
in the current turbulent healthcare environment with high team turnover and less experienced healthcare staff, there has been a nationwide
deterioration in many quality and safety metrics.[35]

Healthcare leaders realize that in the teaming environment discussed in Chapter 4, you must hardwire quality and safety into all
systems and processes. Soon, technology, including artificial intelligence, will be essential in preventing quality and safety issues. In the
interim, educating team members about key performance metrics is

critical. Don't assume that new team members have had quality and safety education. Team leaders need to discuss essential metrics and unit performance. These KPIs (key performance indicators) vary in importance across clinical settings. Examples of key metrics related to nursing care include:

- Patient satisfaction scores
- National patient safety indicators
- Nursing-sensitive outcome measures such as CAUTI, patient falls, pressure ulcers, hours of care per patient day, and ventilator-associated pneumonia
- Hospital-acquired conditions
- Nurse turnover
- Patient throughput

An effective strategy to ensure quality and safety is to create a patient-centered culture in your team. Patient-centered cultures highly value compassion, service, and quality principles. Team members plan their actions and behaviors based on what is best for the patient. The patient experience becomes paramount. Hospitals that don't provide quality patient experiences and quality care struggle with deteriorating reimbursement rates and low scores on the Hospital Consumer Assessment of Healthcare Providers and Systems Survey.[36] The long-term effects of these reimbursement declines can harm a hospital's fiscal health and may make sustaining the mission impossible.

MISSED NURSING CARE

With nationwide staff shortages, units are short-staffed on many shifts. Cary is experiencing this problem in an orthopedic unit where she is a team leader. She remembered as a new graduate that when their team was short-staffed, the experienced nurses on the team told her to skip the baths that day and do "pits and pubes." They were precise with her about what not to do. Her current team is composed primarily of new graduates. They are short-staffed almost every day. These young nurses are deciding what care to stop doing without specific guidance. The unit had two pressure ulcers the previous quarter, something that would never have happened in the past. Cary learned that some nurses had stopped turning patients because they did not have time to complete all their assignments. These young nurses with limited critical thinking skills were deciding what care to skip and sometimes did not make the right choices. Decisions about what care to miss without significantly impacting patients are complex and require critical thinking.

Cary learned through her research that staffing levels, work environment, and teamwork are the most important predictors of missed nursing care. Cary did a missed care assessment with her team looking at the following nine nursing care areas: [37]

- Ambulation
- Turning
- Delayed or missed meals
- Patient education
- Discharge planning
- Emotional support
- Hygiene
- Intake and output documentation
- Surveillance of patients

Cary was stunned that nurses reported missed ambulating and repositioning patients more than 50% of the time. As an orthopedic nurse, she recognized this missed care's impact on patient outcomes. She was also realistic in acknowledging that in the current environment, you could not set the expectation that "everything will get done for patients with no exceptions." Her new strategy when short-staffed was to set three goals for the shift. These goals included the following:

1. We will all leave on time.
2. Everyone is relieved for a break.
3. We don't have time to do the following – here is where she guided what care could and could not be missed.

After evaluating missed nursing care, Cary realized that nurse staffing would be an ongoing challenge in their geographic area. Her organization was open to trying creative solutions to problems. Cary suggested adding exercise physiology graduates from their local university to their orthopedic team. She had met program graduates who worked at her local gym. She learned they knew how to develop fitness and exercise programs to help patients recover from chronic diseases and improve their cardiovascular function, body composition, and flexibility. Their skills were a good fit for the orthopedic team. They could make sure that patients were ambulated and turned. They could also help with range of motion exercises. Her director received the green light to pilot a new mobility technician role in the orthopedic unit. Patients, families, and staff loved the addition of their skill sets. Not only were patients ambulated more consistently, but lengths of stay on the unit decreased as patients became functionally stronger sooner. It was a win-win for patients, staff, and quality of care.

Normalization of Deviance on Teams

Cary implemented significant changes when she recognized the problem of missed nursing care. She is not alone in finding that when she stops for a moment from fighting the fires of staffing and scheduling, she may find that basic policies and practices are not followed. It is a classic example of the normalization of deviance – a growing challenge in many organizations and a significant safety issue. The normalization of deviance is a gradual process in which unacceptable practices or standards become acceptable. As the deviant practices are repeated and taught to new nurses, it becomes the social norm for the team. In today's environment, deviance can arise from a lack of knowledge and close supervision of nursing care.

Research indicates that deviant behavior is just as likely with experienced and inexperienced staff. As nurses become more confident about their judgment, they are more likely to believe they can slightly bend the rules if needed. John Banja cites seven factors that lead to the normalization of deviant behavior in healthcare environments:[38]

1. Staff believe rules are stupid, inefficient, or unrealistic in the current work environment.
2. Staff lack knowledge or may not know the reasons for the practice and procedure.
3. New technologies such as bar code scanning can disrupt ingrained practice patterns, impose new learning demands, or force system operators to devise novel responses or accommodations to new work challenges.
4. Staff believe breaking a rule for the patient's good is OK.
5. Staff believe that rules don't apply because they have experience and can be trusted.
6. Staff fear speaking up when they observe deviant behavior.
7. Leadership is aware of deviant behavior or systems problems, but there is a failure to bring it up the chain of command.

Nurse leaders must commit to patient safety and communicate this to their teams to counter deviant behavior. With medical errors now the third leading cause of hospital deaths, it is problematic when small incremental deviances such as scan overrides occur and become the team norm. Your leadership goal should be to create a team culture of understanding that some practice deviations are likely to happen but that they require swift attention. Staff should feel comfortable speaking up when they see deviant behavior. Preventing the normalization of deviant behavior is an ongoing challenge for leaders and requires continuing diligence. Deviations or rule violations are rarely motivated by malice or greed but often result from nursing staff feeling intense performance pressures.

PROFESSIONAL ACCOUNTABILITY

One challenge with normalizing deviance is that it can lead to team members refusing to accept professional accountability. Professional accountability is crucial to effective teamwork. Without it, achieving trust is challenging because team members are not seen as trustworthy. Professional accountability is doing what you are supposed to do because it is expected of you as a professional or in the role you have taken.[10] Figure 14 illustrates what you can and can't hold staff accountable for.

FIGURE 14

What You Can and Can't Hold Staff Accountable For

Staff Are Professional Accountable For	Things You Can't Hold Staff Accountable For
Maintaining Safe Clinical Practice	Their Life Choices
Adhering to Organizational Policies and Procedures	Organizational Loyalty
Following Through on Commitments Made to Patients, Families and the Team	Being Emotionally Present
Delegating and Supervising Care	Being Unhappy
Maintaining and Upskilling Clinical Competency	Working with Passion
Documenting Care Given	Resignation with Short Notice
Communicating With Others About Patients	Choosing to Unionize
Providing Team Backup	Caring Deeply About Their Work
Respectful Interactions with Others	Mental Health Disabilities Covered by ADA

Scott has accountability issues with his team. He is worried that quality and safety metrics have declined on the unit. When Scott discussed it at a staff meeting, there was a noticeable lack of concern on the part of the staff. Several nurses raised the issue of the organization's poor track record with staff recruitment and retention as the cause of the problems. Some nurses seemed surprised when he pointed out that they could be held professionally accountable for the care given.

Given team turnover during the past two years, Scott realized that many staff did not understand their role expectations. Setting clear goals and expectations is essential to holding your team members accountable. He began a team reset by outlining all role expectations on a document he discussed with each team member and then had them sign it. He also increased the quality and amount of feedback he gave team members. As part of their onboarding, Scott scheduled a meeting with every new team member, including travel staff, to discuss professional expectations. He was wise to realize that staff accountability needed to begin with his leadership accountability.

Incivility and Bullying

Rebuilding a culture of quality and safety often needs to start by examining whether bullying and incivility exist in the team culture. A recent AONL leadership study indicates that 72% of leaders have witnessed bullying and incivility in their environments over the past year. While an increasing percentage of these incidents now involve patients and families, 56% also saw these behaviors among their team members.[39] Bullying and incivility often increase when nurses experience burnout, stress, and anxiety. For some staff, the upswing in public rudeness has normalized bullying behaviors and made it OK to inflict them with no expectation of repercussions.

Renee Thompson is an expert on bullying and incivility in the workplace. She recommends that leaders do a comprehensive assessment before designing interventions when they suspect bullying and incivility.[40] New leaders often make the mistake of jumping into action without full knowledge of all the issues and problems. The challenge is to identify staff bullying behaviors to stop the cycle. Sometimes new staff will see constructive criticism as bullying. There are also differences between staff that are difficult team members and bullies. While difficult staff focus on their needs and wants, the activities of a bully are more directed and intentional. They include the following:

1. **A target** – the bully chooses a target which might be a nurse or a group of nurses, such as new graduates on the unit.
2. **Harmful behavior** – the bully intends to inflict harm through criticism, sabotage, or setting a nurse up for failure. Intent to harm is the difference between constructive feedback and bullying.
3. **Repeated behavior** –the bully repeats the harmful behaviors.

Nurse leaders are responsible for team culture and should watch closely for verbal and nonverbal cues in staff behavior. Some common ones include:

- Talking behind one's back instead of directly resolving conflicts.
- Making belittling comments or criticizing colleagues in front of others.
- Not sharing important information with a colleague.
- Isolating or freezing out a colleague from group activities.
- Snide or abrupt remarks.
- Refusing to be available when a colleague needs assistance.
- Performing acts of sabotage that deliberately set victims up for a negative situation.

- Raising eyebrows or making faces in response to the comments of colleagues.
- Failing to respect the privacy of colleagues.
- Breaking confidences.

A zero-tolerance culture for bullying is the most effective leadership strategy to prevent its occurrence. Team members need education about the behaviors that constitute bullying to help break the silence. Raising the issue at a staff meeting and letting staff tell their stories is crucial in rebuilding a culture. The team needs to know that you will quickly be responsive when you observe bullying behavior or when it comes to your attention. Leaders must engage in self-awareness activities to ensure their leadership style does not support horizontal violence and bullying. Selecting preceptors who support a zero-tolerance policy is critical to orienting new staff about behavioral expectations. Breaking the cycle of bullying on a unit promotes better patient safety. It can help re-energize the team with enthusiasm for their profession and create a healthier work environment.

BULLYING, INCIVILITY, OR ASSAULTS BY PATIENTS, VISITORS, AND FAMILY MEMBERS

Patients, family members, and visitors also sometimes demonstrate incivility and bullying. Charlie is experiencing this issue in the Emergency Department (ED). Because of high patient volumes, wait times in the ED have increased. Patients and families are angrier and often vent their frustrations to the ED team. A patient recently physically assaulted an ED nurse, and she required hospitalization. The ED team is now worried about their safety.

Charlie's experience has grown more common. In a recent pulse survey, ANA researchers noted that an alarming number of nurses report high bullying, incivility, and violence from patients and families in their work settings.[41] Press Gainey researchers found that an average of 57 physical assaults are reported daily by nursing staff. However, this could be the tip of a much deeper iceberg, as many incidents go unreported.[42] Several attacks in 2022 led to the murders of nurses in their workplaces.

Health systems grapple with the uneasy balance between creating excellent patient experiences and protecting the workforce. Many have started crisis prevention intervention (CPI) training, but staff may still feel unequipped to deal with verbal escalation and violent responses. Others are developing codes of conduct, such as that recently adopted by Massachusetts Brigham, where patients and visitors are now required to sign a document outlining disrespectful conduct. These behaviors include:[43]

1. Offensive comments about others' race, accent, religion, gender, sexual orientation, or other personal traits.
2. Refusal to see a clinician or other staff member based on these personal traits.
3. Physical or verbal threats and assaults.
4. Sexual or vulgar words or actions.
5. Disrupting another patient's care or experience.

Violations in the code of conduct may lead to the patient being discharged and having to make other plans for their care and future non-emergency care. Charlie should question his team about specific comments, behaviors, and actions they see from family members or other visitors that are threatening. When making leadership rounds in the ED, he should watch for signs of the following:

- Verbal disrespect of nursing staff.
- Emotional outbursts by family members or other visitors.
- Parents or visitors under the influence of alcohol or drugs.

- Visitation or unit policies that family members ignore.
- Confrontations with staff around issues such as mask-wearing.
- Verbal or physical threats against staff, partners, or other visitors.

AFTER-ACTION TEAM REVIEWS

Charlie took another step with his ED staff after the physical assault on a nurse. He asked his quality and safety department to do an after-action review with the team. The after-action review (AAR) was developed by the United States Army in the 1970s to help soldiers learn from their mistakes and achievements as close to real-time as possible. The use of AARs has expanded into healthcare environments.[44] The goal is to reflect on what strategies were successful and what the pitfalls were. When quality and safety issues occur, it is a simple but powerful way to conduct a post-assessment with your team. Any key learnings from the review are preserved for future knowledge and growth.

A facilitator, not part of the team, led the discussion about the incident with the team using the AAR outline (Toolkit Part 4). The team learned many things from the review. The patient involved in the incident demonstrated very erratic behavior suggesting mental health problems during triage. The triage staff involved were busy and did not share these concerns with other team members. The nurse who was physically assaulted was alone in the ED exam room and turned her back on the patient. Sharp objects, including a scalpel, were within easy reach of the patient. The patient stabbed the nurse without any warning or provocation. The ED team and security response were fast once it became clear what was happening. The nurse was injured, but fortunately, she recovered.

The after-action review led to team communication changes about possible ED environment threats. The examination rooms were recon-figured so no clinician ever turned their back on a patient. It was a recommendation that all team members attend crisis prevention training yearly. As an outcome of the AAR, the team realized that providing security in a hospital now takes a village. Everyone who works needs to be situationally aware that assaults can and do happen. We must train every hospital staff member and volunteer to watch for suspicious behavior or conversations.

Key Points

✓ Team culture significantly impacts many metrics that are now key in healthcare environments and drive payment.

✓ Decisions about what care to miss without significantly impacting patients are complex and require critical thinking.

✓ The normalization of deviance is a gradual process in which unacceptable practices or standards become acceptable.

✓ A zero-tolerance culture for bullying is the most effective leadership strategy to prevent its occurrence.

✓ After-action reviews are a simple but powerful way to conduct a post-assessment with your team when quality and safety issues occur.

REFERENCES – PART 2

1. Stengel C. (ND). Available at https://caseystengel.org
2. Google. re:Work. Withgoogle.com. Published 2011. https://rework. withgoogle.com/print/guides/5721312655835136/
3. Lencioni P. *The Five Dysfunctions of a Team*. San Francisco: Jossey-Bass Publishers; 2002.
4. Covey SM. *Trust and Inspire: How Truly Great Leaders Unleash Greatness in Others*. New York: Simon and Schuster; 2022.
5. Lencioni P. *Overcoming the Five Dysfunctions of Team: A Field Guide*. Jossey-Bass Publishers; 2005.
6. Maben J, Ball J, Edmondson AC. *Workplace Conditions: Improving Quality and Safety in Healthcare*. London: Cambridge Press; 2023.
7. Edmondson AC. Teaming: How Organizations Learn, Innovate and Compete in the Knowledge Economy. San Francisco: Jossey-Bass; 2012.
8. Clark TR. The 4 Stages of Psychological Safety: Defining the Path to Inclusion and Innovation. Oakland CA: Berrett-Kohler Publishers; 2020.
9. Kouzes JM, Posner BZ. The Leadership Challenge 7th Edition. Hoboken NJ: Wiley; 2023.
10. Tye J, Dent B. Building a Culture of Ownership in Healthcare: The Invisible Architecture of Core Values, Attitude and Self-Empowerment 2nd Edition. Indianapolis: Sigma Theta Tau; 2020.
11. Wakefield BJ, Lampman MA, Paez MB, Farag A, Ferguson H, Stewart GL. Delegation of work within a Patient-Centered Medical Home. *Journal of Nursing Administration*. 2022; 52(12):679-684.
12. Campbell AR, Kennerly S, Swanson M, Forbes T, Anderson T, Scott ES. Relational quality between the RN and Nursing Assistant. *Journal of Nursing Administration*. 2021; 51(9):461-467.

13. Walton Family Foundation (2022). *Looking Forward with Generation Z*. Available at https://www.waltonfamilyfoundation.org/learning/report-details-how-gen-z-sees-themselves-and-their-future

14. Polian B. *Coaching and Teaching Generation Z: Honor the Relationship.* Coaches Choice Publishers; 2020.

15. Kar R, Watkinson A, Nelson B. (Gallup Workplace August 31, 2022). How to steer a drifting culture. Available at https://www.gallup.com/workplace/397034/steer-drifting-culture.aspx

16. Tannenbaum S, Salas E. *Teams that Work.* London: Oxford University Press; 2021.

17. Gallup (2023) US Employee Engagement Needs a Rebound in 2023. Available at https://www.gallup.com/workplace/468233/employee-engagement-needs-rebound-2023.aspx

18. Hess V. *6 Shortcuts to Employee Engagement: Lead and Succeed in a Do-More-With-Less World.* Catalyst Consulting LLC; 2013.

19. Bowen W. A Complaint Free World: *The 21-day challenge will change your life; The 21-day Challenge That Will Change Your Life.* London: Virgin Publishing; 2007.

20. Claffey C. Nursing in the dark: Leadership support for night shift. *Nursing Management. 37*(5); 41-44; 2006.

21. Weaver S, Lindgren T G, Cadmus E, Flynn F, Thomas-Hawkins C. Report from the night shift: How administrative supervisors achieve nurse and patient safety. *Nursing Administration Quarterly. 41*(4); 328-36; 2017.

22. AONL (August 2022). Longitudinal Nursing Leadership Insight Survey Part 4: Nurse Leader's Top Challenges and Areas for Needed Support. Available at https://www.aonl.org/resources/nursing-leadership-covid-19-survey

23. Paggi R, Clowes K. *Managing Generation Z: How to Recruit, Onboard, Develop and Retain the Newest Generation in the Workplace.* Fresno CA: Quill Driver Books; 2021.

24. Tutorials Point. The Rule of 7. Available at https://www.tutorialspoint. com/management_concepts/the_rule_of_seven.htm

25. Tulgan B. (August 16, 2016). Communication 101. Available at https://www.td.org/magazines/td-magazine/communication-101

26. Association Healthcare Quality and Research. TeamSTEPPS® Available at https://www.ahrq.gov/teamstepps/instructor/index.html

27. Association Healthcare Quality and Research. Bedside Shift Report Templates. Available at https://www.ahrq.gov/patient-safety/patients families/engagingfamilies/strategy3/index.html

28. Thomas Kilmann Conflict Mode Assessment (ND) available at https://kilmanndiagnostics.com/overview-thomas-kilmann-conflic t-mode-instrument-tki/

29. Johansen ML, Cadmus E. Conflict management styles, supportive work environments and the experience of work stress in emergency nurses. *Journal of Nursing Management, 24*(2), 211-218; 2015.

30. Sandahl P, Phillips A. *Teams Unleashed: How to Release Power and Human Potential of Work Teams.* Boston: Nicholas Brealey Publishing; 2019.

31. Bourke J, Dillon B. (Deloitte Review-January 2018). The diversity and inclusion revolution: Eight powerful truths. Available at https://www2.deloitte.com/us/en/insights/deloitte-review/issue-22/ diversity-and-inclusion-at-work-eight-powerful-truths.html

32. Mind Tools. (ND). Resolving workplace conflict through mediation. Available at https://www.mindtools.com/aj565hn/resolving-workplac e-conflict-through-mediation

33. Gallo A. *Getting Along with Anyone (Even Difficult People).* Boston: Harvard Business Press; 2022.

34. Management Training Institute. (August 1, 2022). Ten tactics for working with difficult people. Available at https://management-traininginstitute.com/10-tactics-for-working-with-difficult-people/

35. Mason G. (February 2022 Becker's Hospital Review) Sharp Drop in patient safety, infection control amid pandemic: 3 new findings.

Available at https://www.beckershospitalreview.com/infection-control/sharp-drop-in-patient-safety-seen-amid-pandemic-3-findings.html

36. CMS HCAHPS: Patients' Perspectives of Care Survey Available at https://www.cms.gov/Medicare/Quality-Initiatives-Patient-Assessment-Instruments/HospitalQualityInits/HospitalHCAHPS

37. AHQR (September 7th, 2019). https://psnet.ahrq.gov/primer/missed-nursing-care

38. Banja J. The normalization of deviance in healthcare delivery *Business Horizon,53*(2); 2010

39. American Organization of Nurse Leaders (October 2022). Longitudinal Nursing Leadership Insight Study. Available at https://www.aonl.org/resources/nursing-leadership-covid-19-survey

40. Thompson R. *Enough; Eradicate bullying and incivility in healthcare, Strategies for frontline leaders.* Incredible Messages Press, 2019.

41. American Nurses Foundation Pulse Survey (July 2022). Pulse on the Nation's Nurses Survey Series: 2022 Workplace Survey. Available at ANA-Pulse-Survey-June-2022.docx (live.com)

42. Business Wire (September 8th, 2022) On Average, Two Nurses Are Assaulted Every Hour, New Press Ganey Analysis Finds. Available at https://www.businesswire.com/news/home/20220908005710/en/On-Average-Two-Nurses-Are-Assaulted-Every-Hour-New-Press-Ganey-Analysis-Finds

43. Mass General Brigham (2022) Patient Code of Conduct. Available at https://www.massgeneralbrigham.org/en/patient-care/patient-visitor-information/patient-code-of-conduct

44. US Army. *The Leader's Guide to After Action Reviews (AAR).* Available at https://www.nwcg.gov/sites/default/files/wfldp/docs/army-leaders-guide-to-aar.pdf

PART 3

BUILDING WORLD-CLASS TEAMS

"Find a group of people who challenge
and inspire you, spend a lot of time with
them, and it will change your life."

AMY POEHLER

CHAPTER 11

CREATING A SENSE OF COMMUNITY

Chris had a very cohesive team before the COVID pandemic. Her staff had worked together for years and knew one another well. If one team member had a personal life crisis, the group came together to help. Chris doubted she could have gotten through her husband's unexpected death five years ago without the support of her team. The team delivered food for her family, and someone checked on her daily. She marveled at the level of team connection that made an experience like that happen and now mourns the loss of it. Today, the nurse turnover on her team has skyrocketed. Nurses don't know each other well. A sense of community is lacking in the group. Everyone seems focused on their needs and does not consider the impact of last-minute call-ins on team functioning.

Chris is not alone. Nurse leaders are discouraged by the turmoil in the healthcare environment and the impact on the nursing work-force. Most tell me they see no easy path forward. Gallup researchers now warn that there has been a shift in an employee mindset, and it will become more challenging to establish a sense of community and teamwork in the workplace.[1] In a situation like this, setting a few goals to move the needle in a more positive direction can be helpful. One goal I often recommend is to work diligently on establishing more solid connections and a sense of community between your new staff and other team members. Most of what we discuss in this chapter costs little but time.

Feeling connected is something that is missing on most nursing teams today. Many nurses feel like they no longer matter as individuals on their teams. There is an endless churn of travelers on some nursing teams. Recent graduates join teams and don't feel part of anything special – making it easy to leave with few regrets. Seasoned nurses don't invest in new nurses because they assume most will be short-timers. Nurse managers acknowledge that they barely know the names of new staff. Environments become psychologically unsafe because the stage of inclusion safety is not present. Christine Porath, a researcher in civility, reminds us that we have a choice even if we feel overworked. You can master civility, connect with others and bring humanity back into the work environment.[2]

This lack of team connection has made many nurses feel dispensable and believe their organization does not value their well-being. US Surgeon General Vivek Murthy issued an advisory calling for workplaces to protect employee mental health. He points out in this work that part of the "essentials" for well-being at work is *mattering,* a belief that you are valued and essential to others.[3] For some staff who live alone, team relationships are especially significant as they may not regularly interact with others outside of work.

Without feeling a connection, leaving a team becomes an easy decision for team members. There is a universal human need to feel seen and valued by those around us. In research by McKinsey, Generation Z workers were found to be more disconnected, with a higher likelihood of mental health problems when compared to other generations in the workplace.[4] We will never overcome the recruitment and retention challenges or improve teamwork without fixing the disconnectedness. When teams fall apart, they must be rebuilt. Restoring connectedness will not happen without careful planning. A full-court focus on building connections among team members is the place to start.

REBUILDING FRIENDSHIPS ON TEAMS

When Chris asked her team about their relationships with others on the team, very few of them reported having a friend at work. It is a question on the Gallup Q12 employee engagement survey. Gallup has found that staff with a best friend at work are more engaged and less likely to leave. New Gallup research demonstrates that having a best friend at work matters more today than ever. For many employees, the pandemic caused traumatic experiences and other profound difficulties, particularly for healthcare and other frontline workers and educators.[5] These employees found the social and emotional support from their best friends at work to be more critical than ever to get them through these challenging times. Having a best friend at work can help us navigate the turbulent environment that we are in today and allow us to check our assumptions about our environment.

As they looked at ways to build connections, Chris's team launched several initiatives. These included:

The Battle Buddy Program - is designed to forge relationships between new staff based on an initiative developed by the US Army. The New York City Hospital System was the first healthcare organization to pilot the program. Battle buddies help each other through difficult situations and stop nurses from self-isolating when things become challenging. The Army learned that even forced friendships are better than no friendships.[6]

A New Nurse Welcome Package - is sent to nurses' homes before their first day. The welcome package includes a piece of clothing (hat or shirt) with the logo of the nursing team. Chris's team has seen Instagram or TikTok postings made by staff who receive them which is an additional plus for recruitment.

Meet our New Staff Board – before their arrival, information about new staff is placed on the new staff board in a breakroom or lounge with pictures and critical information about the new staff joining the team.

A Team Volunteer Program – the team chose the Boys and Girls Club as their first volunteer effort. They bought five unassembled bicycles. They decided on a weekend day/time to build the bikes as a team. It was an excellent teambuilding session where staff spent time with each other outside the work environment. Those that could not take time off to build the bikes designed gift bows and delivered them to the Boys and Girls Club.

RE-ESTABLISHING TEAM RITUALS

As Chris's team looked to rebuild their sense of community, they realized that during COVID, nurses did not have group lunches or take breaks together. The group did not celebrate special events like baby showers, birthdays, and retirements. Given the lack of rituals, it is unsurprising that team members feel disconnected from each other. These social rituals play an essential role in the workplace by doing the following:

- They help us learn about each other on a personal level.
- They help connect us as a team.

- They help new team members feel psychologically safe and included in the workplace.
- They provide opportunities for us to give each other recognition.
- They lead to higher team retention.

The significance of rituals is captured in the book *Rituals Roadmap* by Erica Keswin, who points out that rituals are an evidence-based practice of building more cohesive teams.[7] When rituals are lost, our connections to one another become weaker. Rituals like celebrations or meals revitalize us in ways other things don't. Keswin defines a ritual as a sequence of repeated symbolic actions over time formalized into the fabric of team culture to maintain group cohesion. Rituals help build psychological safety because they promote team inclusion. Rituals can reinforce an organization's values and make staff feel part of something special. Without them, teams struggle to build meaning in their work, and little social glue holds the team together.

Any ritual started should add value, enhance feelings of psychological safety and improve performance. An excellent place to start redesigning your rituals is to ask staff for their ideas. Younger staff may want different new traditions than a more seasoned workforce. Some areas to rebuild rituals include the following:

- Nurse recognition and the celebration of Nurse Week
- The onboarding of new staff
- Reflections at the beginning of meetings or shift huddles
- Team meals and snacks in breakrooms
- Social events outside of work
- Charity walks and community fundraising drives
- Professional development and achievement, such as certification

A Team of Net Promoters

Healthcare systems are spending millions of dollars to recruit and retain staff. But what if your team undermines some of those efforts? Consider the experience Jeff had at his local gym. He overheard two nurses talking about their hospital, a local competitor. In loud voices, they were trash-talking about the organization and its leaders. It made Jeff wonder whether some of his critical care team might be doing the same thing. As a teambuilding exercise, he measured the ICU staff's net promoter score quarterly using a pulse survey. When you think about it, his idea makes sense. Younger nurses regularly use online ratings to make decisions about products and services. They are more likely to value a rating or recommendation from a friend about an excellent place to work versus outreach from your recruiter.

Net promoter scores are a widely used market research metric that typically takes the form of a survey question asking respondents to rate the likelihood that they would recommend a company, product, or service to a friend or colleague.[8] It is also part of the HCAHPS patient satisfaction assessment. A net promoter score for nurse recruitment can be done organization-wide or at the unit level by asking how likely you are *to recommend nursing employment to your friends and colleagues on this unit (or in this organization)*. The question should use a Likert Scale of 1-10 from very unlikely to very likely. The net promoter score is calculated by evaluating how many staff fall into each of the following categories:

Promoters (9-10) are your most engaged and satisfied team members who promote employment in your organization.

Neutral (7-8) – these team members may be content to stay themselves but are not likely to promote the organization to their colleagues or friends.

Detractors (1-6) – these team members are unhappy and disengaged. They won't recommend employment to other nurses and may even discourage others from applying, as those nurses in the gym story above.

Jeff did an anonymous net promoter assessment which gave him the average score for the unit by breaking down the number of nurses in each group. He calculated the employee net promoter scores by deducting % of detractors from your % of promoters. He ignored those who scored 7-8 or the passive staff. The results are on a percentage scale from 1 to 100. Jeff found that 30% of the ICU staff are promoters, and 20% are detractors. The ICU's net promoter baseline is 10%. He now has a baseline and shares the data with staff. Jeff was disappointed because companies like Apple have NPS scores in the 70s.

After collecting the data, Jeff asked his team: *"It is 3rd quarter, and our net promoter score is 70%. To achieve that, what would need to be true on our team that is not true today?"* The staff had many ideas for an improvement plan. Although an employee NPS can measure success, it's only significant compared to a previous score or another organization's results. On its own, it can't tell you much. But it is an excellent place to start. Nurses listen to other nurses, especially in the current environment. If your team is not promoting your organization, the most expensive recruitment strategies will not likely work.

PROMOTING COLLABORATION ON TEAMS

Carly accepted a clinical leader position on a unit that had just implemented a team-based care model. Her team included new graduate RNs, virtual nurses working in offsite centers, patient care technicians, and licensed practical nurses. She observed that each team member seemed to work independently of one another despite their new care model. They did not function as a team or seem to find value in collaboration.

There was no identity as a team. Carly realized the lack of team identity impacts individual behavior and team interactions.[9] Together, they could be much more effective in meeting the needs of patients, but collaboration would need to occur first. She needed to clarify that team collaboration is essential and establish expectations. As Carly learned, even the best teams aren't great on day one. They grow, adapt and adjust over time. If the staff has not had experience with great teamwork, they might not value it the way she does. In a sense, you must see it before you can be it.

Cooperation and collaboration are essential to getting the work done, especially in a team-based care environment. Team collaboration is the cornerstone of building team synergy because collaborative teams work together, share knowledge, and manage challenges. Carly talked with the team about some fundamental tenets that are important to team collaboration, such as:[10]

- If we work together, we will more effectively conquer the challenges than we could as individuals.
- There are no winners and losers on a team. Everyone plays a unique role, and everyone matters.
- We focus on each other's strengths and don't call out weaknesses.
- We assume good intentions before jumping to conclusions about the motivations of others on the team.
- We are all accountable for our patients and don't use language like – "That is not my patient."
- We focus on what's right and not who's right.

Collaborative teams also demonstrate some important attributes described in earlier chapters of this book, such as:[11-12]

- **Clarity:** Clear communication is critical. While your team may not agree on everything, you must communicate opinions, ideas, and priorities to avoid unnecessary conflicts or misunderstandings.

- **Efficiency:** How collaborative your team is does not necessarily correlate with how much time they spend together. It's all about how time is utilized. Keep meetings or huddles short and to the point to help your teammates finish their work on time.

- **Positivity:** Not all shifts will go smoothly. Teams who can shake off challenging days and start the next shift with a positive attitude make collaboration a long-term success.

- **Trust:** Your team members need to feel safe if you want them to contribute their ideas and unique skills. Ensure your team knows you have their best interest at heart and believe in their abilities.

- **Accountability:** Check in with your team and make sure everyone is holding themselves accountable for their work—if someone's missing deadlines or not delivering the expected quality of work, try to locate the issue and support them with team backup.

Carly recognized that without a strong team identity, the team would not successfully deliver team-based care. Chapter 12 will discuss how team leaders can promote and teach teamwork skills.

Key Points

✓ A lack of team connection has made many nurses feel dispensable and believe their organization does not value their well-being.

✓ Having a best friend at work can help us navigate the turbulent environment that we are in today and allow us to check our assumptions about our environment.

✓ Rituals help build psychological safety because they promote team inclusion.

✓ Net promoter scores are a widely used market research metric that typically takes the form of a survey question asking respondents to rate the likelihood that they would recommend a company, product, or service to a friend or colleague.

✓ A lack of team identity impacts individual behaviors and team interactions.

CHAPTER 12

TEACHING TEAMWORK SKILLS

Willie is an ambulatory surgical center nursing director with a team of seasoned staff and many new graduates. He feels like he is watching the musical West Side Story play out daily on his team. The musical explores forbidden love and the rivalry between the Jets and the Sharks, two teenage street gangs of different ethnic backgrounds. There is little that the gangs agree on, just like Willie's staff, who have very different ideas about team loyalty and team backup. Willie's seasoned staff complain that new graduates are late in setting up rooms and rarely reach out to help others in the group. The younger staff complain that older staff are judgmental and have weak technological skills. In response, seasoned nurses complain about newer nurses who "treat the screen" and not the patient.

In Chapter 6, we discussed generational ideas about teams and teamwork. Generation Z staff have yet to gain experience with teamwork and are more self-oriented in their work. Team members need to value their differences to work effectively. Recent Press Ganey data indicates that effective teamwork, which is so essential to a culture of safety, is a metric where health systems have seen the most marked drops in the last three years.[13]

Willie knows that putting the staff together on a team does not always lead to effective teamwork. There are skills that staff need to learn, especially today. The only way to develop community and cohesiveness among your teammates is to get them together professionally and personally. He started the conversation at a staff meeting by asking his team to talk about the most incredible team they had ever been on and a follow-up question about what made the team great. His staff spoke about the following:

- We took time to learn each other's strengths and weaknesses.
- Everyone played a role in the team's success.
- We could have difficult conversations.
- We laughed about our different viewpoints.
- We got through rough times together.
- We communicated with each other.

Willie pointed out that they needed to learn both teamwork skills and great teammate moves to have the kind of special team experience they discussed. Each staff member was asked to share their answers to the following questions:

To bring out the best in me, the team should

_____

_____

Things that I don't do well that the team should know about include

_____

_____

Something I can bring to the team to make us more effective is

_____

_____

When staff discussed their answers to these questions, Willie noticed that the team climate had changed. Everyone identified their strengths and challenges and how they could support the team. He moved the discussion from "me" to "we." They began to think more like a team, and while having a team-first mindset would be their goal, these conversations were a good start. All team members should contribute to the team in ways that add the most value. Being a strong team leader means putting your staff in positions where they can excel.[12]

Teaching Team Backup

Leaders are sometimes surprised that some team members don't have a natural inclination to provide team backup to others. Janine discovered that when she joined a rehabilitation unit team as a leader. The unit adopted a Blended Care Team Model first piloted by the Allegheny Health System, including RNs, LPNs, and PCTs.[14] When team members arrived in the morning, they swiped their ID badges to check in and automatically swiped **No Meals** assuming they would have no break coverage. Janine was surprised by this because break coverage was one of the cornerstones of the Blended Care Model. She investigated what was happening on the team and found each staff member working alone on their assignment. They lacked a team mindset which defeated the purpose of the new care model.

Janine's concerns are understandable. Strong team backup should be a core value for the team and one that all team members reinforce. Janine started teaching team backup as part of the assignment process. Every staff member had a covered break time on the schedule and an assigned backup buddy. When team members came to her with challenges, she asked if they had discussed the problem with other team members urging them to do that as a first step. She also talked about the concept of good teammate moves, which include the following:

- Answering the call lights in rooms not assigned to you.
- Offering to help with a complex patient admission.
- Relieving a nurse so they can take a break.
- Helping another staff member at the end of the shift.
- Offering to take a new patient even though it is not your turn.

Two other initiatives that managers have discussed with me as strategies to reinforce team backup include:

The Emergency Pit Crew – when complex patients are admitted, the emergency pit crew approach is adopted to facilitate that patient's timely admission and treatment. Team members drop everything and go in and help so no one gets behind or overwhelmed.

No Team Member Left Behind – team leaders assess whether everyone is on track with their work at least an hour before the shift ends. Tasks are reassigned when needed, so everyone leaves on time.

TEAMWORK RECOGNITION

It is often the little things in teams that lead to big successes. Recognizing and calling out great teamwork is significant. Team recognition also matters. Allan is a team leader in a burn unit. This unit's teamwork skills are essential because caring for patients requires strong team backup. Patients are admitted to the regional burn center on an emergency basis, and the initial care is complex and time-consuming. Victims range in age, and some of the stories are heartbreaking. It is emotionally draining work, and a strong work support system is essential.

Allan contributes to his team's performance evaluations completed by the unit manager. He notices staff are not rated on their teamwork skills. Allan found this problematic because some nurses are not team players. There is an adage that what gets measured gets done. Recognizing excellent teamwork skills became a high priority for Allan. At the end of every shift huddle, he does a shout-out for something each staff member did to demonstrate outstanding teamwork, such as:

- Dale – thanks for keeping us all on track when things became chaotic in the unit.
- Sonia – thanks for taking the admission when it wasn't your turn, but you were the best person to do it given your skill level.
- Tally – thanks for ordering lunch, keeping all the orders straight, and using your Venmo account for us to pay you.
- Kassie – thanks for not bursting into tears when you admitted that young baby, although I know you felt like doing so. You helped all of us manage our emotions.

Allan also decided to nominate his team for the DAISY Team Award™. This award recognizes that while an idea to achieve better patient and family outcomes may start with one individual, it often takes an entire team to implement successfully. The DAISY Team Award™ is designed to honor collaboration by two or more people, led by a nurse, who identify and meet patient and patient family needs by going above and beyond the traditional nursing role.[15] The criteria include the following:

- Teams must be led by a nurse or a group of nurses.
- Teams must be comprised of two or more individuals.

- Team members exemplify your organization's values and embody your mission.
- Team members are role models of collaboration and teamwork that make a difference.in patients' lives, families, employees, and the community.
- The team's project should be described in detail, including outcomes.

Although it was hard to choose one example, Allan reviewed the patient nominations of burn unit nurses. He decided the team had been at its best when a young couple was admitted to the burn unit after an automobile accident. Their burns were quite severe, but both were expected to recover. As the team worked together to admit the two patients, they learned the couple had a golden retriever puppy at home. They were understandably stressed about what would happen to the dog. The couple was new to the area and had no one to turn to. Allan's team sprang into action. They contacted the landlord with the couple's permission and were able to enter the apartment. One of the team picked up the dog while the rest worked out a fostering plan so the puppy would receive the care he needed. The team members rotated, fostering the puppy. They arranged Facetime calls so the couple could see their dog and took cute videos and pictures. Seeing their dog brought joy and hope during a very challenging time. The dog was not allowed to visit the burn unit but visited the rehabilitation center after both patients were transferred for further treatment. Allan doubted the couple would have made the progress they did without knowing their dog was safe and cared for.

REMOTE TEAMWORK SKILLS

A growing number of nursing teams either work remotely or have at least a few team members who work remotely. Some teams can have periodic face-to-face interactions, but this is not always possible. Finding a way to build an inclusive team with remote staff is more challenging. New care models that include virtual nurses must provide mechanisms to build strong communication and collaboration between onsite staff and those working virtually.

An early adopter of virtual nursing was the Catholic Health Initiatives in Colorado which implemented a Virtual Integrated Care Team Model. In this model, five key roles for the virtual nurse were identified: [16]

- Patient education
- Staff mentoring and education
- Real-time quality/patient safety surveillance
- Physician rounding
- Admission and discharge activities

Their experience indicates that it takes time to build trust and confidence with the "new" virtual member of the bedside care team. The hardwiring of role responsibilities and including evidence-based practice protocols are essential for program success. In Chapter 6, we talked about role clarity. The CHI model evaluation indicates this is crucial in successfully implementing virtual nurse models.

Building teamwork when all members are entirely remote is even more challenging. Connection, communication, and culture are essential building blocks in remote teamwork. Eliana's virtual team of case managers initially struggled to be cohesive. Eliana did not have the luxury of face-to-face meetings because the team covered a wide geographic area. The group met weekly using Zoom as their meeting platform. While the technology was good, Elaina noticed that the case managers did not use the web cameras provided to them. The meetings were a screen of black boxes with little interaction from the case managers. The case managers did not know each other well, and the meeting agendas offered little time for social interaction.

Eliana knew that building a cohesive remote team would involve resetting the team norms and rebuilding teamwork skills. The first problem the team needed to discuss was using webcams. There are two types of team cultures: webcams on cultures and webcams off cultures. Engagement is higher when webcams are on. Team meetings are far more interactive, and information is more clearly communicated. Opting out of being on camera should not be an option. It also prevents embarrassing moments that Eliana experienced several times when she called on a case manager with their webcam off, who did not answer and may not have even been in the room.

The new team norm was that webcams would be turned on and kept on throughout their meetings. She kept the meetings to one hour, and the agenda went out in advance. Case managers could add to it. Eliana expected team interaction and often stopped for questions and comments. Eliana also took time at the beginning of the meeting for teambuilding activities. She made personal updates part of her recurring meetings. Instead of just jumping into the agenda, the team did a check-in about their week, rating it on a scale of 1 to 10, with ten being a great week. This activity helped the team better support those who had a challenging week as they shared their highs and lows. She also built-in activities to help the case managers learn more about each other such as:

- A fun fact about you.
- Two truths and a lie – guess the lie I am telling about myself.
- The color of my personality free assessment. [17]

Interprofessional Team Skills

In team-based care models, the care delivery team works with members of other disciplines to plan and coordinate patient care, especially in areas like discharge planning. Effective communication and collaboration across disciplines are essential. No one should be able to opt out of participation in activities like interprofessional rounding or discharge planning meetings.

Maurice manages a surgical unit. The lengths of stay in his department have increased. Before the pandemic, their interprofessional meetings were robust, and everyone attended. That all fell apart in the COVID environment when the rounding stopped. Getting it restarted has been a challenge. His nursing team members feel too busy to participate in rounding, and the surgeons believe it wastes their time. Maurice feels a sense of urgency because volumes in his medical center are high, and moving patients across the continuum of care is a crucial priority.

Maurice realizes that many of his current staff and the surgical physicians are new and may not see the value in this rounding. Every discipline has a unique culture, language, and mental model for approaching patient situations. Professionals are often surprised about the knowledge and clinical abilities of other disciplines. This respect may not happen initially but does grow over time. We can sometimes assume that professionals will see the value in interdisciplinary teamwork without being explicit about the benefits. To practice effectively in an interprofessional care environment, one must clearly understand other members' unique contributions, educational backgrounds, areas of high achievement, and limitations. Maurice knows that he will need to model the way and help nurses and physicians see the value in collective knowledge and talents by soliciting varied viewpoints on patient situations when planning care for patients.

Key Points

✓ Generation Z staff have yet to gain experience with teamwork and are more self-oriented in their work.

✓ Strong team backup should be a core value for the team and one that all team members reinforce.

✓ The DAISY Team Award™ is designed to honor collaboration by two or more people, led by a nurse, who identify and meet patient and patient family needs by going above and beyond the traditional nursing role.

✓ Finding a way to build an inclusive team with remote staff is more challenging.

✓ Effective communication and collaboration across disciplines are essential.

CHAPTER 13

FOSTERING EMOTIONAL INTELLIGENCE

Over the past three decades, the importance of a leader's emotional intelligence has been widely recognized. It was popularized in 1995 by Daniel Goleman with the publication of his best-selling book *Emotional Intelligence*.[18] Emotional intelligence (EI) is self-mastery or the ability to understand and control what we feel (our emotions) and the way we act (our response to these emotions). There are four components to emotional intelligence:

- **Self-awareness** – You recognize your emotions and how they affect your thoughts and behavior, know your strengths and weaknesses, and have self-confidence.

- **Self-management** – You can control impulsive feelings and behaviors, manage your emotions healthily, take the initiative, follow through on commitments, and adapt to changing circumstances.

- **Social awareness** – You can understand other people's emotions, needs, and concerns, pick up on emotional cues, feel comfortable socially, and recognize the power dynamics in a group or organization.

- **Relationship management** – You can develop and maintain good relationships, communicate clearly, inspire and influence others, work well in a team, and manage conflict.

Increasingly, we also see that these same concepts apply to teams.[19] Team members should be mindful of the emotions of their members. Team emotional intelligence (EI) refers to the ability of a team to recognize and manage emotions in themselves and others effectively. High levels of team EI can help teams work more effectively and efficiently, leading to improved outcomes and stronger team performance. Teams with high levels of EI are typically more cohesive, able to handle stress and change effectively, and work well together to achieve common goals. On the other hand, teams with low levels of EI may struggle with conflicts and communication breakdowns, leading to decreased productivity and poor performance.

Low levels of team emotional intelligence were problems that Trevor experienced with his staff. While the team's internal relationships should be the glue that holds the group together, team members were often in conflict with little concern about the impact of their behaviors on their teammates. During a recent conflict mediation he was involved in, one staff member told the other, "*This is who I am -so deal with it.*" Trevor recognized that promoting emotional intelligence is more challenging now when things have become increasingly divisive. Researchers who study emotional intelligence find that it is on the decline.[20] The increasing use of social media is thought to play a role as more interaction happens online instead of face-to-face.

Team Education About Emotional Intelligence

Given society's declining emotional intelligence, leaders like Trevor struggle to foster it in their teams. The first step is to educate staff about team emotional intelligence. EI is a collective responsibility and requires team members to prioritize the group's emotions and social interactions. Teams with high EI think about the impact their behaviors and actions will have on the group. For example, negativity is a strong emotion and can quickly influence team dynamics and relationships. Moods, both positive and negative, can quickly spread throughout the team. Some additional strategies that Trevor can use include the following:

1. Ask the team about the role that emotions play in their team interactions.
2. Discuss the role of stress on teams and how to manage it collectively.
3. Set team norms and ground rules.
4. Use the circle of influence to discuss what the team can and cannot control.
5. Be proactive in discussing any "elephants in the room" that the team may not be surfacing. Ask, *"What is the real issue here?"*
6. Encourage more open communication and honesty and ask for points of disagreement.
7. Use coaching questions such as – *"What impact do you think your words (or behaviors) have on other team members?"* or *"Have you brought that concern up in the team huddle?"*
8. Work with the team in practicing active listening and empathy.
9. Encourage frequent check-ins with other team members to see how they are doing and if they need help.
10. Inspire team members to be authentic and take responsibility for how their behavior and words land on others.

Helping a team to achieve a higher level of emotional intelligence takes intentionality. To be most effective, the team needs to create emotionally intelligent norms—the attitudes and behaviors that eventually become habits—that support behaviors for building trust, group identity, and group efficacy.

Teaching the Team to Think Again

As Trevor learned, managing group emotions can be challenging. How team members think about things can quickly become habits they don't bother to question. Telling another team member that "this is just who you are" means that you are not staying open or curious about how others perceive situations. In *Think Again: The Power of Knowing What You Don't Know,* Adam Grant, a University of Pennsylvania organizational psychologist, investigates rethinking in three areas—the individual, changing others' minds, and collective environments.[21] Learning to reconsider their beliefs is an essential skill for teams to learn to build emotional intelligence. Grant points out the value of doubt and how we can better embrace the unknown and gracefully accept when we are wrong. He also believes it is helpful to understand the following about human nature:[21]

- Most of us favor the comfort of conviction over the discomfort of doubt.
- The smarter you are – the more problems you may have in updating your beliefs.
- Once we accept information as accurate – we rarely bother to revisit it. Things don't become true just because you believe them.
- Under acute stress – team members revert to their automatic, well-learned responses. As we sit with beliefs, they become more, not less, entrenched.

- Most of us defend our beliefs using one of three modes – the preacher (who supports sacred beliefs even in the face of new information), the prosecutor (who focuses on attacking new ideas), or the politician (whose views are swayed by what others think).
- We all have "totalitarian egos," whose job is to keep out threatening information. Most people have a binary bias – linking complex continuums of beliefs into two extremes.

Team learning should be about evolving collective beliefs, not affirming them. Rethinking starts with "intellectual humility," or acknowledging what you don't know. When we let our views and opinions, such as "*This is who I am,*" become our identity, any assault on our worldview threatens our sense of self. As a leader, Trevor should not be a logic bully with his team by overwhelming them with information to support ideas they are not ready to hear. Instead, he could begin by asking highly individualistic team members how they formed their viewpoints. Listening is a crucial skill in negotiation, as is a willingness to point out valuable observations made by others. Learning to rethink is a skill set that can lead to more effective teamwork in an ever-changing world. It is not always easy to do, but it's learnable.

UNDERSTANDING THE WORK STYLES OF OTHERS

Alexis is trying to promote emotional intelligence with her team in the Pediatric Intensive Care Unit. An area that the group has struggled with is social awareness. She has several team members who believe they work harder than the rest of the staff and share these beliefs regularly. Alexis realizes that part of the problem is a lack of understanding of the different work styles on the team. Some nurses like control and are very task driven. They have a low tolerance for the feelings, attitudes, and advice of others. Other nurses on the team are more relationship-driven.

They spend more time communicating with patients and prioritize their work differently.

Alexis decided to have each team member do the IHI Work Style Inventory, which helps identify a preferred or dominant work style.[22] The goal was to learn about yourself and work more successfully with others. Alexis wanted the staff to appreciate that diversity in work styles would help build a stronger team. The four primary work styles in the IHI model are outlined in Figure 15.

FIGURE 15

IHI Work Styles

Analytical	Driver	Amiable	Expressive
Detail Oriented	Independent + Competitive	Excels at Gaining the Support of Others	Comfortable with Risk and Spontaneity
Want Structure + Organization in Work	Want Control and Ability to Take Decisive Action	Enjoy Close Personal Relationships	Loves Generating New Ideas
Enjoy Task Oriented Work	Low Tolerance for Feelings, Attitudes and the Advice of Others	Works More Slowly – Making Sure the Team is Cohesive	Struggles with Follow Through
Less Team Oriented Seeks Security	Frustrated by the Inaction of Others	Supportive and Thoughtful Wants Security + Inclusion	Works Quickly and Excitedly with Others

---

This exercise was helpful for Alexis's team. About half the group were either analytical or drivers in their approach to work, and the rest had an amiable or expressive approach. Using the IHI guide, the team reviewed each work style and the tips for working with others.[22] Alexis tackled the issue that some in the group thought they worked harder than others. She pointed out that some team members are more task-focused depending on their work style, and others worry about relationships. Having this diversity in work styles and approaches among team members would avoid the possibility of Groupthink. Groupthink is a psychological phenomenon that occurs within teams when a push for conformity can ultimately result in incorrect or flawed group decision-making outcomes. Group members try to minimize conflict and reach a consensus without critically evaluating alternative ideas or viewpoints. Cognitive and work style diversity is not encouraged. Alexis explained that for the team to succeed, they need to be open to other team members' ideas and approaches to their work.

STRENGTHS-BASED TEAMS

Another strategy to build emotional intelligence in teams is to know and encourage each staff member to use their strengths and talents. Investing in strengths can have a significant payback on the level of team engagement. When team members use their strengths, Gallup research indicates they are six times more engaged in their work and 7.8% more productive in their roles.[23] Historically, performance management models and most leaders have focused on fixing staff weaknesses or deficits. While managing weaknesses to meet role expectations does matter, part of the joy of being human recognizes that we are all different and have unique gifts.

Everyone has strengths and weaknesses. When coaching teams, Gallup research has found that the world's greatest leaders report that they don't waste their time focusing on employee weaknesses but instead work to draw out their talents. This approach is counterintuitive to what most leaders believe when they have the same expectations for all their staff in every area. For example, some of your team members may be naturally gifted teachers and make excellent preceptors, while others are not.

Ideally, you would use talent assessments such as the Clifton Strength Finders ® [24] to learn about the unique gifts of your team. If this is not available, leaders can observe their staff to learn about their natural talents and ask some good open-ended questions such as:

1. What do you do best in your role?
2. What do you enjoy most about the work you do every day?
3. What comes naturally to you in your work that others struggle with?
4. What are some of the things you do in your work that you receive compliments about?
5. What do you look forward to doing each day at work?
6. What hobbies do you have outside of work?

These questions will give the nurse leaders insight into the natural talents of their team members. When you know a staff member's strengths, you can individualize your approach in assignments and other activities to enhance the work experience.

KEY POINTS

✓ Emotional intelligence (EI) is self-mastery or the ability to understand and control what we feel (our emotions) and the way we act (our response to these emotions).
✓ Teams with high levels of EI are typically more cohesive, able to handle stress and change effectively, and work well together to achieve common goals.
✓ Team learning should be about evolving collective beliefs, not affirming those that may no longer serve us well.
✓ The IHI Work Style Inventory helps team members identify their preferred or dominant work style and those of others.
✓ An important strategy to build emotional intelligence in teams is to know and encourage staff to use their strengths in their work.

CHAPTER 14

RECRUITING AND RETAINING TEAM MEMBERS

As discussed in Chapter 1, the healthcare recruitment and retention landscape in the United States is challenging and will be in the future. The gap between the number of nurses needed and those available continues to grow as demand for healthcare services increases. Healthcare staff is in the driver's seat with many choices and employment opportunities. Leaders are frustrated because recruitment has become very transactional, with less focus on long-term opportunities within employment settings or benefits and more attention on hourly pay. Younger staff seek employment with a "tour of duty" mindset discussed in Chapter 4, with most staying less than two years in units where they initially accept the job.

Yet despite these realities, the concepts related to teamwork and establishing a sense of community among staff discussed in this book become even more essential to long-term staff retention. With shorter tenures on teams, organizations are shifting from a focus on retention at the unit level to organizational retention. Innovative organizations now develop flight plans for their new staff, demonstrating how to achieve their career goals within the health system. Career coaches and coaching are now more commonplace. Some organizations even hold yearly nursing drafts where staff can request transfers to other specialty areas to hardwire their commitment to internal mobility.

With 52 being the median age of a nurse in the United States, wise nursing leaders realize that we must keep seasoned nurses in the workforce as long as possible.[25] Glide paths for nurses between the ages of 55 and 65 are in place in some health systems. Seasoned staff is often a core part of virtual staffing models and models designed to provide new graduates with clinical coaching. The healthcare workforce demands more flexibility in scheduling, so concepts like a Nurse Seal Team [26] and internal travel agencies are also emerging.

Frontline nurse leaders also recognize that retention begins with recruitment. Their involvement in the recruitment process is critical. The interview is an excellent place to set the stage for a conversation about the importance of feedback discussed in Chapter 8 to the professional growth of staff. The interview is also a time to talk about the realities of the workplace. In his book, *The Millennial Whisperer,* Chris Tuff observes that many young employees don't work in high school today. Their first job may be with you. Pointing out that you will love about 70% of your work in any job and dislike about 30% is essential.[27] There are no Instagram-perfect jobs. In today's marketplace, even when a staff member accepts a position, it does not mean they stop their job search. Staying connected with staff from the job offer to their first day of employment is essential.

RECRUITING TEAM PLAYERS

Our focus in this book has been on the importance of teamwork in healthcare and in redesigning care delivery models. Yet we know that not all nurses are team players; some don't want to be. Seth had this challenge with his urgent team. As he talked with his staff about teamwork and team backup, Seth realized that he had nurses who did not buy into the value of teamwork. These nurses were good clinically but did not see the merits of teamwork. Seth made it clear that teamwork was something that they could not opt out of but also realized that he needed to recruit with teamwork in mind. Seth's decision is a good one. Questions about teamwork should be asked as part of the interview process if the goal is to hire nursing staff who will become strong team players.

Assessing teamwork skills during the interview process can be tricky. Some attributes of good team members include the following:

- Respectful of others' time, boundaries, and ideas.
- Willing to prioritize team needs over personal needs.
- Keeps commitments to team members.
- Does not engage in gossip or drama.
- Communicates frequently and does not blindside others.
- Maintains a positive outlook.
- Provides team backup to others.

In the Chapter 4 Toolkit, we have interview questions to assess the candidate's experience with teamwork and whether they value it. Some sample questions included in that guide are:

1. How has teamwork helped you accomplish something you could never have achieved yourself?
2. What actions and support, in your experience, make a nursing team function successfully?
3. Have you been on a nursing team that struggled or failed to work effectively together? What do you assess as the reasons for the failure?

4. What do you do consistently in your practice to provide team backup to other team members?

5. How do you manage conflicts with other team members?

Onboarding New Team Members

Once a position is offered and accepted, the next step is onboarding. Onboarding is a comprehensive process where new employees transition into new roles and become part of your organization. Onboarding usually occurs at least two levels in every organization. The first level is at the hospital or health system level, where staff orients to the mission, culture, electronic health record, key policies, and procedures. Some organizations then have a general nursing orientation which could include a competency or skills assessment. The final level of onboarding is at the unit or department level, where new staff meets their team members.

This adage still holds: *"You never get a second chance to make a first impression."* Attention to excellent onboarding at all these levels is crucial because it forms critical first impressions. New hires who experience a poorly planned and executed orientation may conclude that the organization is not well managed and decide that it was a mistake to take the job. Research from the Society for Human Resource Management (SHRM) indicates that a great onboarding experience produces the following outcomes:[28]

- Higher job satisfaction
- Organization commitment
- Lower turnover
- Lower stress
- Higher performance levels

You should have four primary goals (the 4 Cs) when onboarding new staff, as outlined in Figure 16.

FIGURE 16

The 4Cs in Onboarding New Staff

Confidence	Build the confidence of the new staff member in his/her ability to do their job.
Connection	Establish meaningful connections and relationships with other members of the team (inclusion and safety).
Culture	Educate the new staff member about the culture, values and expected behaviors.
Clarity	Provide clarity about role expectations, communication norms and career opportunities.

Nurse leaders should ask new staff members about their onboarding experience. Check what happens with the staff–preceptor relationship if that is part of your onboarding. Some nurse preceptors are burned out from onboarding so many new team members and may not be making the investment they once did. Unfortunately, nurse managers sometimes delegate these responsibilities to preceptors or unit educators without follow-up.

Charisse had not been following up with new employees. She thought things were going smoothly with orientation on the unit she managed but then received feedback that there were issues with onboarding. Recent graduates received a thorough orientation as part of their residency, but the transition for more experienced nurses was hit or miss depending on the unit workload. She interviewed several recent new nurse hires and received critical feedback about crucial elements that seemed to be missing from orientation. Leaders should have regular check-ins scheduled at the end of the first week and the conclusion of the orientation experience. Examples of questions to ask on check-in include the following:[26]

1. Has our team made you feel welcome?
2. Did you receive what you needed to begin work? (e.g. Benefits information, ID badge, keys, email, and EMR access)
3. Do you have questions that have not been answered?
4. What challenges do you see in your new role?
5. Can we change anything to help new staff better adjust to the unit?

During check-ins with new staff, Charisse learned that her current team was not effectively connecting with new employees. To strengthen the connection, she designed a meet-the-staff scavenger hunt like the ones she used for equipment and supplies. She asked each staff member to give her a question that they would like to be asked by new employees. Some staff chose work-related questions, but most were about hobbies and pets. New staff had four weeks to complete the scavenger hunt. Clarisse saw an immediate improvement in connecting new and existing team members by formalizing the process.

INTEGRATING TRAVEL NURSES

Travel nurses will be part of core team staffing for the foreseeable future. Managers should value the experience and adaptability that travelers bring to a group. A downside is that if not integrated into the team, nursing staff may get angry about travel pay, and the travel nurses could recruit your current staff. A successful experience for a travel nurse is contingent on good onboarding and ongoing communication about performance expectations. A good relationship with the nurse manager is an essential bridge to socializing travel nurses into the organization and a factor in the nurse's decision-making to extend a contract if requested.[29]

Some important **DOs** when travel nurses join your team include the following:

1. **Embrace the travel nurse as a welcome addition to your unit** – Choosing to be a travel nurse has tradeoffs. It can be lonely when you don't feel anchored to one location. Your staff may not know travel contracts can be terminated with little notice and that the advertised pay is not what most receive.

2. **Ensure travel nurses are oriented** – Orientation is needed even at this time with streamlined onboarding. Make sure your travel nurses know whom to go to with their questions.

3. **Set role expectations** – Leaders should set clinical role expectations with travel nurses. Additional expectations could include the traveler refraining from discussing their salaries with staff and not serving as a travel agency recruiter.

4. **Check in with your travel nurses and seek feedback** – Many nurses working on travel contracts are highly experienced and have worked in some of the country's best healthcare systems. Why not use their expertise? Ask them what is going well in the unit and where improvement is needed. Seek information about best practices that have seen work in other settings.

5. **Include your travel nurses in celebrations and parties** – Some travel nurses will not be at home for holidays. Include the travel nurses in unit gatherings and nurse recognition celebrations. Too often, they are left out of these events, making it harder for them to feel like team members.

6. **Make them net promoters** – Some travel nurses regularly share their travel experiences with large audiences on social media sites like Instagram and TikTok. When experiences with a team and unit are good ones, their endorsement can be significant. Always

ask great travelers what it would take to get them to join your team. Some are looking for a home and don't plan on traveling for the rest of their careers.

Stay Interviews

Retaining team members today is very challenging. Leaders become frustrated when staff resigns, and they later learn they might have stayed in the organization with minor changes. You won't know unless you ask. Not surprisingly, the practice of STAY interviews is gaining momentum. It is considered a best practice in staff retention. Leaders conduct these interviews to understand why employees stay and what might cause them to leave. It also gives nurse leaders insight into what matters most to their staff. In an effective STAY interview, managers ask structured questions casually and conversationally. The goal is to collect real-time information on what matters most to nurses and then individualize your retention strategies. The following five questions are important ones to ask:[30]

Question 1: What do you look forward to each day at work?
This question brings nurses into the here and now and asks them to focus on their daily duties and challenges rather than expand on broader issues like pay and benefits. Employees stay and engage based on their relationships with supervisors and colleagues and how much they like what they do. These factors are often more important than pay and benefits.

Question 2: What are you learning here, and what do you want to learn?
This question helps leaders to direct their career coaching. Some nurses are ambitious to advance, some are curious to learn more, and others want to work and go home.

Question 3: Why do you stay here?

While appearing simple at first, this question opens doors for discovery about retention. Many staff have never thought about this, so the leader's role is to help them reflect. You might follow this first question with a second question about whether that was the only reason or whether they have other reasons.

Question 4: When did you consider leaving us last, and what prompted it?

Everyone thinks about leaving a position at some point, so a directly worded question brings a much-needed conversation into the light.

Question 5: What can I do to make your job better for you?

This question casts a wide net for all remaining topics. Some responses may be challenging to hear. Avoiding defensiveness is critical. Be transparent about what you have influence over and areas that you may not.

STAY interviews with staff should be done early in the first year and then yearly. Look for themes in staff answers, especially questions three and four, which can alert you to environmental risks. Stay interviews also help identify factors that keep employees in the organization, known as job embeddedness factors. Understanding these factors can be essential for your recruitment efforts. I encourage residency program coordinators to do STAY interviews with new graduates at their transition's 30, 60, and 90-day points. Nursing research done by Versant suggests that at every point they survey in the first two years, many nurses consider leaving but feel the organization could have intervened.[31]

Ila, a residency program coordinator, began doing STAY interviews with her health system's new graduates. She learned that in the first 90 days, some recent graduates were already considering leaving the organization. One key issue that new nurses talked about was their inability to navigate conflict with their team members. They lacked the confidence to have these conversations and saw leaving as the only way to reduce stress. Ila built a conflict management module into the residency program, including simulated exercises on mediating conflict. The new graduates gained confidence, and Ila realized she would never have known about the challenge had she not conducted the interviews.

STRATEGIC OFFBOARDING

Historically, nurse leaders have heard that staff don't leave their organizations; they leave leaders. Today, nurses leave positions for many reasons, including a desire for higher pay, work flexibility, and feelings of burnout. Resignations are inevitable, even for the best leaders, but never easy. Many managers dread when staff walks into their office and says, *"I need to talk with you about something."* They fear that *something* will be a resignation, and sometimes it is.

A wise mentor once told me that a resignation should be viewed in some ways, like a funeral. *"How you behave,"* she observed, *is a tribute not only to the person leaving but to everyone left behind on the team."* I have always found this to be good advice. Once a staff member has decided to resign, regardless of how inconvenient it is for you as the manager, how you behave says a great deal about you as a leader. It impacts how honest employees will be with you if they consider other career opportunities and whether they see you as someone supporting professional growth. Leaders who feel that a resignation indicates disloyalty acquire a reputation as angry and vindictive. Your leadership behaviors should include the following:

- Acknowledge their contributions to the team and that they will be missed.
- Ask if there is anything you can do to change their mind (if you want to).

- Work with them on a transition date and inform them of any benefits they are entitled to.
- Keep the lines of communication completely open.

Many employers now have active strategies to stay in contact with staff who have left and invite them back. This practice is called strategic offboarding. Offboarding is the process used by an organization to formally separate a nurse after resignation, termination, or retirement.[32] There is a strong business case to turn valued departing employees into loyal alums using a holistic approach to offboarding.

Kelly, a critical care manager, once spent little time with staff who had resigned other than to thank them and wish them good luck. She has now completely changed her approach. Kelly has observed that some of her nurses sometimes want to try new things, believing the grass is greener elsewhere. Others move to travel positions, usually with specific financial goals, such as paying down debt or saving for a home down payment. She shifted focus to turn valued team members who leave into loyal alums who are net promoters for her unit. She has also realized that a few may want to return at some point.

When valued staff leave, Kelly now stays in touch with them via social media or text. She recently did this with a nurse who accepted a position with a local competitor for a sign-on bonus. The nurse immediately texted her back and thanked Kelly for reaching out to find out how she was doing. The nurse told Kelly she missed her old team and wondered if she could work one day per diem in the critical care unit. Kelly was delighted to bring her back per diem and understands that doing this sends a strong message to her current team that the unit is a great place to work. How you manage staff who leave speaks volumes about your leadership. If you lose a staff member, remember that it does not have to be forever, as Kelly did. Great supportive leaders are unfortunately in short supply, but staff often don't realize this until they leave, so leave the door open.

KEY POINTS

✓ The current healthcare recruitment and retention landscape in the United States is challenging and will continue to be in the future.

✓ Attention to excellent onboarding at all these levels is crucial because it forms critical first impressions.

✓ Travel nurses will be part of core team staffing for the foreseeable future. Managers should value the experience and adaptability that travelers bring to a group.

✓ STAY interviews are a best practice for staff retention.

✓ Many employers now have active strategies to stay in contact with staff who have left and invite them back. This practice is called strategic offboarding.

CHAPTER 15

PROMOTING TEAM WELL-BEING

Even before COVID-19, there was great concern about the stress and burnout healthcare staff reported. In the whitepaper, *The IHI Framework for Improving Joy in Work*, the authors noted that if burnout in healthcare were described in clinical or public health terms, it might be called an epidemic.[33] Fast forward to today's healthcare environment, and the stress, exhaustion, and burnout levels among staff have escalated.

Every healthcare discipline and department now feels the pressure of surging volumes, increased service demand, and staffing shortages. In a recent advisory, the Surgeon General of the United States noted: *"So many health workers have been able to persevere and perform despite those conditions is a testament to our training, our teammates, and the ideals that have called us to serve. But day after day spent stretched too thin, fighting against ever-increasing administrative requirements, and without the resources to provide our patients and communities with the care they need, have driven many nurses, doctors, community health workers, and public health staff to the brink."*[34]

The long-term impact of COVID-19 on the healthcare workforce is something that researchers will likely study for years to come, but there is a mounting concern. New evidence indicates that the experience with COVID has had a devastating impact on our youngest nurses. Nurses' mental health and well-being are the top challenges reported by leaders in a recent AONL study.[35] These concerns are well-founded. Organizations are finding that the traditional methods of promoting well-being are not working in the current environment. Some nurses won't use employee assistance services out of fatigue or to avoid stigma. Many healthcare staff resent the word "resilience" and resist education about resiliency strategies. Talking about resilience implies that the staff member lacks something they should have. Healthcare environments are turbulent and short-staffed. Clinicians feel burnout and moral distress because they cannot always provide the care patients need and deserve. Maintaining resiliency today is exceptionally challenging.

WELL-BEING

Discussions about how to help healthcare teams have moved beyond resilience and wellness strategies to promoting well-being. There is a difference between wellness and well-being. Gallup researchers define wellness as describing a healthy lifestyle beyond acute illness. It refers to a state of physical health in which people have the ability and energy to do what they want without chronic suffering. In contrast, well-being encompasses the broader holistic dimensions of a well-lived life. Although there are other definitions, Gallup's global research team has found the following five elements of well-being that add up to a thriving life:[36]

- **Career well-being:** You like what you do every day.

- **Social well-being:** You have meaningful friendships in your life.

- **Financial well-being:** You have enough resources and manage your money well.

- **Physical well-being:** You have the energy to get things done.

- **Community well-being:** You like and feel connected to others where you live.

There is a strong business case for team well-being outside of it just being the right thing to do. Most of the healthcare workforce will be either Generation Z or Millennials by 2025. In research published by Gallup, organizational commitment to well-being is the number one factor in employment selection by Generation Z and Millennials. [36.] A focus in this area is now a crucial differentiator for organizations that want to be employers of choice. Based on their well-being research, Gallup experts now recommend that organizations evaluate their net-thriving score at the individual, team, and organization levels. You can measure the well-being of team members by asking a powerful two-part question that captures many well-being factors. The answers will determine the individual's average Gallup Net Thriving (GNT) score — revealing if the staff member is suffering, struggling, or thriving. The two key questions to ask and scale (Figure 17), according to Gallup research, are: [36]

1. Imagine you are on a staircase with ten steps, ten being the best possible life – What step are you on today?
2. Imagine five years from now. What step will you be on?

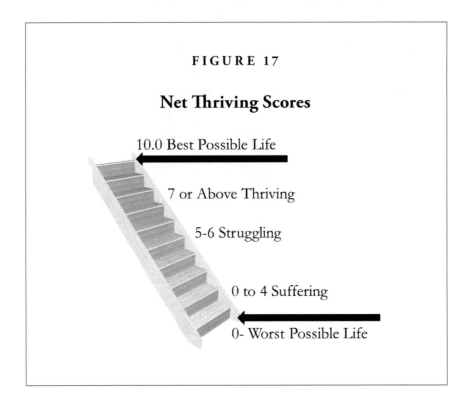

FIGURE 17

Net Thriving Scores

10.0 Best Possible Life

7 or Above Thriving

5-6 Struggling

0 to 4 Suffering

0- Worst Possible Life

TEAM COACHING FOR WELL-BEING

Dorie used the Gallup net-thriving questions with the emergency department team. Scores for her team members ranged from a low of three to
a high of nine. The team average was 6.0. She saw noticeably different
scores by age group. Team members under 35 trended with much lower
scores. This data was consistent with pulse surveys by the American
Nurses Association, in which nurses under 35 were far more likely to
evaluate themselves as not or not at all emotionally healthy.[37]

Dorie coached each of her team individually, asking, *"To move to the
next step on this ladder, what would need to be true that is not true today?"*
She was surprised that the answer was not always what she expected. Some
staff talked about their lack of sleep or inability to decompress after work.
For others, the answers involved different aspects of well-being, such as

feeling lonely when not at work or financial issues. Dorie realized that while what happens at work is critical to well-being, other determinants in one's life also matter, as outlined in the Gallup model. She took the time to learn about the well-being benefits offered by their organization so she could provide help in a broader range of areas, such as financial planning. Some additional coaching questions she used with her team included:

- How can we support each other to raise our team's net-thriving score?
- What are examples of strategies that have worked before to get us through hard times?
- How things can we stop ruminating about as a team that is in our circle of concern but not our circle of influence?
- What strengths does this team have that could help us in this turbulent time?
- How are we growing as a team during this challenging time?

As Dorie discussed well-being with her team, she realized she was also very burned out. Other frontline nursing leaders share feelings similar to hers about their emotional health. Leaders like Dorie have been shock absorbers for their staff as they frame the many challenges in their work environments. Many of her staff have high anxiety, stress, and clinical depression. She now finds herself coaching team members experiencing emotional meltdowns and panic attacks. These conversations can sometimes be heartbreaking and have taken a toll on Dorie.

To destigmatize seeking help, Dorie sought mental health counseling that was part of their employee well-being program. She found it highly beneficial in reframing some of her stress and anxiety. The counselor pointed out that Dorie was not setting boundaries around her work and was often in touch with her staff 24/7. The lack of decompression from work was causing her to have emotional distress and burnout. She talked with staff about her counseling experience and hoped her role modeling would help her team seek help.

Social Determinants of Work Health

Justin Montgomery is a nursing director in the Dartmouth Hitchcock Health System. In a webinar discussion about well-being, he noted the following in the chat, *"Much like we know that improving health is not happening solely by interactions with healthcare, rather it's better handled by addressing Social Determinant of Health; our ability to retain staff means addressing their work environment AND the Social Determinants of their Work Health. That's challenging and different."* Like Dorie in the case above, Justin realized that his team does not leave their problems at home when they come to work.[38]

We often overlook our nurses' social determinants of work health and wonder why our retention strategies are not working. Social determinants of work health are the conditions nurses are born into, grow up in, go to school in, live in, and work in that shape their work health. For nurses, social determinants of work health could include factors such as:

- Level of student loan debt
- Safety/crime in the geographic area where one works
- Availability of childcare
- Access to healthy food while working
- Household debt
- Support systems in the community
- Cost of living in the geographic area
- Housing costs
- Access to public transportation and parking
- Caretaker for family members
- Stressful events such as births, divorces, or deaths
- Engagement and a sense of belonging in one's community

Suppose I am a new graduate who has accepted a night nursing staff position in a major city. I may be coping with a long commute, high rents, parking challenges, concerns about safety on nights/weekends, a high student loan burden, and social disconnection from others on my work team. Without support and help, I may decide what had seemed like an exciting first job is, instead, very stressful on many levels. I may see myself as never getting ahead in this setting. Like many in my age group, I will look at travel roles to explore less expensive geographic areas, pay down debt and live in paid housing. These strategies may help me to feel more in control of my life and time. Much like in healthcare, where we know how social determinants can impact health outcomes and risks, our retention strategies or efforts to maintain a healthy work environment may not be enough without looking at a given nurse's social determinants of work health.

Healthy Work Environments

We end this book with a discussion about healthy work environments. Building an effective work team is contingent on having a healthy work environment. The American Association of Critical Care Nurses is committed to promoting the creation of healthy work environments. They identified six standards for establishing and sustaining healthy work environments in their now widely used work. These include:[39]

1. **Skilled communication** – A nurse's proficiency in communication is as important as clinical skills.
2. **True collaboration** – Nurses must relentlessly pursue and foster collaboration.
3. **Effective decision-making** – Nurses must be valued and committed partners in making policy, directing and evaluating care, and leading organizational operations.
4. **Appropriate staffing** – Staffing must effectively match patient needs and nurse competencies.

5. **Meaningful recognition** – Nurses must be recognized and recognize others for the value that each brings to the organization's work.

6. **Authentic leadership** – Nurse Leaders must fully embrace the imperative of a healthy work environment, authentically live it and engage others in its achievement.

There is growing evidence in the nursing literature about the positive impact of healthy work environments on team culture, staff well-being, retention, and better patient care. Many organizations have launched efforts to improve their work environments. Achievement of Magnet designation is considered the gold standard for hospitals seeking to build healthy professional practice environments that support nurses' work. Findings from an increasing body of nursing research have provided evidence supporting that Magnet® hospitals have increased patient and nurse satisfaction, improved recruitment and retention of nurses, and improved patient outcomes.

Although there are now national discussions about what needs to happen in practice environments to maximize nurses' health and well-being, achieving these standards has proved challenging for many organizations. The gap between nurse supply and demand keeps growing. All of these standards become harder to achieve without adequate team staffing. The future of the healthcare workforce's well-being is contingent upon redesigning how we deliver care. In his advisory, the Surgeon General noted that when he visits healthcare settings today and asks staff how they are doing, they tell him they are exhausted, helpless, and heartbroken. Collectively they agree that something needs to change.[34]

FINAL THOUGHTS

Undoubtedly, we will soon see the emergence of many innovative team-based models of care. A significant change, such as a redesign of care delivery, often happens gradually at first, then the momentum rapidly shifts. We have no choice. We can't keep doing what we are doing and expect better outcomes. Outside of a few specialty areas, future care delivery models will necessitate a team-based approach with professionals and support staff all working at the top of their scope of practice. There is power in teamwork, and teams will generally outperform individuals. Teamwork is an essential part of the infrastructure needed to execute new models of care. Yet most frontline leaders will tell you that it has weakened and will need to be taught and nurtured. When you bring together healthcare staff with complementary skills, a shared purpose, and mutual accountability, a synergy develops that can overcome even the most significant challenges. I hope this book will serve as a toolkit and practical guide to fostering effective team-based care delivery regardless of your clinical setting.

KEY POINTS

✓ Discussions about how to help healthcare teams have moved beyond resilience and wellness strategies to promoting well-being.

✓ There is a strong business case for team well-being outside of it just being the right thing to do.

✓ Well-being encompasses the broader holistic dimensions of a well-lived life.

✓ We often overlook our nurses' social determinants of work health and wonder why our retention strategies are not working.

✓ When you bring together healthcare staff with complementary skills, a shared purpose, and mutual accountability, a synergy develops that can overcome even the most significant challenges.

References – Part 3

1. Gallup Research (2023) Managing the biggest leadership issue of our time. Available at https://www.gallup.com/workplace/469790/culture-shock.aspx?utm_source=workplace&utm_medium=email&utm_campaign=culture_shock_book_announcement_email_1_03152023&utm_term=press&utm_content=learn_more_textlink_1

2. Porath C. Mastering Community: The Surprising Ways Coming Together Moves Us from Surviving to Thriving. Essex: Balance Publishing; 2022.

3. US Surgeon General Advisory (April 2022) Addressing healthcare workforce burnout: https://www.hhs.gov/surgeongeneral/priorities/health-worker-burnout/index.html

4. McKinsey (January 14th, 2022). Addressing the unprecedented behavioral challenges facing Generation Z. Available at https://www.mckinsey.com/industries/healthcare/our-insights/addressing-the-unprecedented-behavioral-health-challenges-facing-generation-z

5. Patel A, Plowman S. (Gallup Workplace August 17th, 2022). The increasing importance of having a best friend at work. Available at

6. https://www.gallup.com/workplace/397058/increasing-importance-best-friend-work.aspx

7. Sherman RO. (Emerging RN Leader September 2nd, 2021). Creating a Battle Buddy Program. Available at https://emergingrnleader.com/creating-a-battle-buddy-program/

8. Keswin E. *Rituals Roadmap: The Human Way to Transform Everyday Routines into Workplace Magic.* New York: McGraw-Hill; 2021.

9. Davies J. (September 17th, 2020 Qualtrics Blog) What is employee net promoter score (eNPS) and how can it be used to improve employee engagement? Available at https://www.qualtrics.com/blog/employee-net-promoter-score-enps-good-measure-engagement/

10. Widdowson L, Barbour PJ. *Building Top Performing Teams: A Practical Guide to Team Coaching to Improve Collaboration and Drive Organizational Success.* London: Kogan Page; 2021.

11. Sandahl P, Phillips A. *Teams Unleashed: How to Release Power and Human Potential of Work Teams.* Boston: Nicholas Brealey Publishing; 2019.

12. Maben J, Ball J, Edmondson AC. *Workplace Conditions: Improving Quality and Safety in Healthcare.* London: Cambridge Press; 2023.

13. Maxwell JC. *The 17 Indisputable Laws of Teamwork.* New York: Harper Collins; 2001.

14. Lee TH. *Healthcare's Path Forward: How the Ongoing Crises Are Creating New Standards for Excellence.* New York: McGraw-Hill; 2023.

15. Zangerle C. (Marcus Evans CNO Summit February 23rd, 2023). Evolving Care Models: Bringing LPNS Back to the Bedside.

16. DAISY Team Award. Information Available at https://www.daisy-foundation.org/daisy-award/team-award

17. Cloyd B, Thompson J. Virtual nursing: The wave of the future. *Nurse Leader.* 18(2) 147-150; 2020.

18. The Color of My Personality. Free Assessment. Available at https://thecolorofmypersonality.com/

19. Goleman D. *Emotional Intelligence*, New York, NY, England: Bantam Books, Inc.; 1995.

20. Greaves J. *Team Emotional Intelligence: The Four Essential Skills of High Performing Teams.* TalentSmart; 2021.

21. Fugere M. (Psychology Today Blog -November 13th, 2021). Why Emotional Intelligence is on the Decline. Available at https://www.psychologytoday.com/us/blog/dating-and-mating/202111/why-emotional-intelligence-is-in-decline

22. Grant A. *Think Again: The Power of Knowing What You Don't Know.* New York: Viking Press; 2021.

23. Institute for Healthcare Improvement. (2019 Publication). Work Styles Inventory Worksheet. Available at https://www.

ihi.org/education/IHIOpenSchool/resources/Pages/Activities/
Duncan-WorkingStyle.aspx

24. Gallup (ND) Why Create a Strengths-Based Company Culture.
Available at https://www.gallup.com/cliftonstrengths/en/290903/
how-to-create-strengths-based-company-culture.aspx

25. Gallup Clifton Strengths Finder Available at https://www.
gallup.com/cliftonstrengths/en/home.aspx?utm_source=-
google&utm_medium=cpc&utm_campaign=us_strengths_
branded_cs_ecom&utm_term=clifton%20strengths&
gclid=Cj0KCQjw2cWgBhDYARIsALggUhpaKdHZ5iwiamRBA9VO2l-
uE4vscw_CYXSF4tsv_RQ985WuwYjDCtH8aApK9EALw_wcB

26. National Council State Boards of Nursing. 2020 National Nursing
Workforce Study. Available at https://www.ncsbn.org/research/
recent-research/workforce.page

27. Thum A, Fortner T, Hudson D. Building a Dynamic, Flexible
Nursing Workforce: The Jefferson SEAL RN Team. *Nurse Leader*.
21(1). 51-55; 2023.

28. Tuff C. *The Millennial Whisperer*. New York: Morgan James
Publishers; 2019.

29. SHRM Guide. Onboarding New Employees. Available
at _foundation_ourwork_initiatives_resources-from-past-
initiatives_Documents_Onboarding%20New%20Employees.pdf

30. Hansen A, Tuttas C. Lived Travel Nurse, and Permanent Staff
Nurse Pandemic Work Experiences as Influencers of Motivation,
Happiness, Stress, and Career Decisions: A Qualitative Study. *Nursing
Administration Quarterly*. 46(3). 245-254; 2022.

31. HR Soft. The Stay Interview Kickstart Guide. Available at https://
www.scribd.com/document/418746504/Stay-Interview-Kick-Star
t-Guide-HRsoft-pdf

32. Africa L, Trepanier S. The role of the leader in reversing intent to
leave. *Nurse Leader*. 19(3). 239-245.

33. Dachner AM, Makarius, EE (March/April 2021). Turning departing employees into loyal alumni: A holistic approach to offboarding. *Harvard Business Review. Available at* https://hbr.org/2021/03/turn-departing-employees-into-loyal-alumni

34. IHI Joy In Work Whitepaper. (2017). Available at https://www.ncha.org/wp-content/uploads/2018/06/IHIWhitePaper_FrameworkForImprovingJoyInWork.pdf

35. Surgeon General Advisory (April 2023). Addressing Health Worker Burnout. Available at https://www.hhs.gov/sites/default/files/health-worker-wellbeing-advisory.pdf

36. AONL Longitudinal Leadership Insight Study (2022) Available at https://www.aonl.org/resources/nursing-leadership-covid-19-survey

37. Clifton J, Harter J. *WellBeing at Work: How to Build Resilient and Thriving Teams.* Gallup Publishing; 2021.

38. ANA Pulse Survey (2022). Third Annual Survey. https://www.nursingworld.org/practice-policy/work-environment/health-safety/disaster-preparedness/coronavirus/what-you-need-to-know/annual-survey--third-year/

39. Justin Montgomery (Webinar with Dartmouth-Hitchcock December 3rd, 2021). *Become the Leader No One Wants to Leave: Nurse Recruitment and Retention in Turbulent Times.*

40. American Association of Critical Care Nurses. Healthy Work Environment Model. Available at https://www.aacn.org/nursing-excellence/healthy-work-environments

PART 4

THE TEAM BUILDING TOOLKIT

"Not finance, not strategy. Not technology. It is teamwork that remains the ultimate competitive advantage, both because it is so powerful and rare."

PATRICK LENCIONI

TEAM ASSESSMENT

Use a Likert Scale of 1-5 to evaluate each of the following statements:

1 = Strongly Disagree
2 = Disagree
3 = Neither Agree nor Disagree
4 = Agree
5 = Strongly Agree

Sense of Belonging on this Team

1. I feel I am an essential member of this team.
   1   2   3   4   5
2. Our team has trusting and supportive relationships.
   1   2   3   4   5
3. New team members are warmly welcomed.
   1   2   3   4   5
4. I offer my help when other team members need it.
   1   2   3   4   5
5. I am willing to make sacrifices for this team.
   1   2   3   4   5

The score for this team member   _____

Team Backup

1. My team members encourage one another.
    1   2   3   4   5
2. The team works cooperatively to get work done.
    1   2   3   4   5
3. We share information needed to get the job done.
    1   2   3   4   5
4. We help each other resolve problems.
    1   2   3   4   5
5. Bullying and incivility are not tolerated on the team. 1
    2   3   4   5

The score for this team member   _____

Communication on this Team

1. Our team frequently communicates during the shift.
    1   2   3   4   5
2. I consult other team members for their opinions.
    1   2   3   4   5
3. Communication is open and honest on the team.
    1   2   3   4   5
4. Team members seek out and give feedback.
    1   2   3   4   5
5. We can effectively manage conflict as a team.
    1   2   3   4   5

The score for this team member   _____

<u>Work Division</u>

1. Assignments are made fairly on this team.
   1 2 3 4 5
2. I am comfortable questioning an assignment.
   1 2 3 4 5
3. When short-staffed, we know what we can omit.
   1 2 3 4 5
4. When busy, we all work together to leave on time.
   1 2 3 4 5
5. We understand each other's strengths.
   1 2 3 4 5

The score for this team member   _____

<u>Recognition on the Team</u>

1. We thank one another on this team.
   1 2 3 4 5
2. Teamwork is rewarded in our organization.
   1 2 3 4 5
3. We celebrate each other's achievements
   1 2 3 4 5
4. I am proud to work on this team.
   1 2 3 4 5
5. Team members are supportive of one another
   1 2 3 4 5

The score for this team member   _____

After assessing individual scores, you can also add the scores in each category for an average team score.

Adapted from team research conducted by <u>Airline Cabin Crew Team System's Positive Evaluation Factors and Their Impact on Personal Health and Team Potency</u> Youkyung Ko, Hwaneui Lee, Sunghyup Sean Hyun Int J Environ Res Public Health. 2021 Oct; 18(19): 10480. Published online 2021 Oct 6. doi: 10.3390/ijerph181910480

A SWOT Analysis of Our Team Culture

	Promotes Teamwork	Harmful to Teamwork
Internal to the Team	**Strengths** • What do we do well? • How cohesive are we as a group? • Do we have a good skill mix on the team? • What are our most significant accomplishments? • Are our team members net promoters of the team? • How well do we know each other? • Do we assist each other when needed? • Does our team have rituals? • Do we have consistent leadership?	**Weaknesses** • Do we tolerate bullying and incivility? • Do we have a high rate of turnover on the team? • What knowledge, skills, and talents are we missing on this team? • What areas do we need to improve in as a team? • Are nurses on our team committed to being team members? • What patient complaints have we had about our team?
External to the Team	**Opportunities** • What actions can we take to be a more cohesive team? • How can we take advantage of what is happening with the nursing workforce? • How can we use our academic partnerships to build more cohesive nursing teams? • What can we do to highlight and recognize teamwork in our unit?	**Threats** • What challenges might we face with staffing shortages moving forward? • How can we minimize using travel nurses who are harder to integrate into the team? • Are there things happening in our health system that could negatively impact us as a team? • Do we have competitors out there offering benefits that might impact our turnover?

HELPING YOUR TEAM WITH CRITICAL THINKING SKILLS

What is Critical Thinking?

A simple definition of critical thinking is that it is reasonable, reflective thinking focused on deciding what to believe or do. In nursing, critical thinking for clinical decision-making is the ability to think systematically and logically. Evidence shows leaders can coach team members to become better critical thinkers. A team with strong critical thinking can do the following:

- Remain open-minded and mindful of different alternative actions.
- Prioritize what matters most in clinical situations.
- Judge the credibility of the evidence.
- Ask appropriate clarifying questions.
- Explain reasons for actions taken
- Seek second opinions from other members when unsure about clinical judgments.

Coaching Questions to Promote Critical Thinking

1. **To Organize Care** – How will our team plan care for these ten patients? What should our first actions be?

2. **To Clarify Thinking** - What do we think the issue is here as a team?

3. **To Inspire Reflection** - Why do you think the team was successful in that situation? Could we have used another approach?

4. **To Challenge Assumptions** – How do we know that our assumptions as a team are correct in this situation? Is there another way to view this problem?

5. **To Build Accountability** – Based on our team's experience, what do you suggest we do here? What changes would be in the best interest of our patients right now? How could we have managed this situation differently? What would great look like now (if a service recovery issue with a patient)?

6. **To Develop a Growth Mindset** – What would we as a team do here if we knew we could not fail? How could this situation help the team to grow? What have we learned about ourselves as professionals?

© 2023 Rose O. Sherman

After-Action Team Reviews for Quality and Safety Problems

The United States Army developed After Action Reviews (AARs) in the 1970s to help soldiers learn from their mistakes and achievements as close to real-time as possible. The use of AARs has expanded into healthcare environments. The goal is to reflect on what strategies were successful and what the pitfalls were. When quality and safety issues occur, it is a simple but powerful way to conduct a post-assessment with your team.

Formal reviews are ideally conducted by a facilitator, not part of the team with a stake in the outcome. The discussion should occur as soon as possible when the incident has occurred. They are best-done face-to-face.

Key Questions asked during an after-action review include:

1. **What did we expect to happen?**
2. **What occurred?**
3. **What went right? What went wrong?**
4. **How could we have better anticipated this outcome?**
5. **What could we improve upon, and how?**

Ideally, most time focuses on what can be improved moving forward and how. The overall goal is organizational learning for future growth and knowledge. Discussion ground rules could include the following:

1. Focus on learning rather than grading success or failure.
2. Recognize that there is always room for improvement.
3. Share honest perceptions without the assignment of blame.
4. Understand that no one has all the information or answers.
5. Participate actively in the discussion.

6. Accept that everyone's views have value.
7. Be open to new ideas.
8. Seek consensus where possible.
9. Use a "yes, and" approach
10. Don't quote individuals without permission.

A well-conducted after-action review should include actionable recommendations to improve team processes and decision-making.

Adapted THE U.S. ARMY'S AFTER-ACTION REVIEWS: SEIZING THE CHANCE TO LEARN (2000). Available at https://www.nwcg.gov/sites/default/files/wfldp/docs/army-seizing-chance-to-learn.pdf

Using the Circle of Influence with Your Team

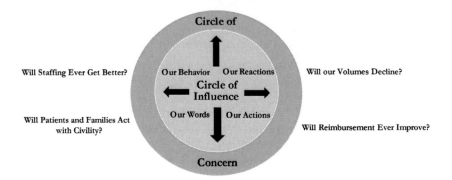

Will Staffing Ever Get Better?

Will Patients and Families Act with Civility?

Circle of

Our Behavior   Our Reactions

Circle of Influence

Our Words   Our Actions

Concern

Will our Volumes Decline?

Will Reimbursement Ever Improve?

1. Is this issue we are discussing in our circle of influence or circle of concern?
2. What can we do within our circle of influence to impact this situation?
3. How could implementing that behavior increase our circle of influence in this situation?
4. What do we know we could be doing in this situation but are not yet taking action?
5. What could be the consequences here if we fail to change our behavior?

The Circle of Influence comes from the work of Covey SR. *The 7 Habits of Highly Effective People 30th Anniversary Edition.* New York: Simon & Schuster; 2020. It is a way of reframing challenging discussions to evaluate what the team has control over and what it does not. Dr. Covey recommended that teams focus their energy on what falls directly in their Circle of Influence to reduce stress.

INTERVIEW QUESTIONS TO ASSESS TEAMWORK SKILLS

Teamwork is essential in healthcare, where no single team member can accomplish high-quality patient care in any clinical environment. Yet we know that not all nurses have strong teamwork skills, and some don't want to be team players. Questions about teamwork should be asked as part of the interview process if the goal is to hire nursing staff who will become strong team players.

Assessing teamwork skills during the interview process can be tricky. Some attributes of good team members include the following:

- Respectful of others' time, boundaries, and ideas.
- Willing to prioritize team needs over personal needs.
- Keeps commitments to team members.
- Does not engage in gossip or drama.
- Communicates frequently and does not blindside others.
- Maintains a positive outlook.
- Provides team backup to others.

Some questions that can provide insight into how the applicant views teamwork and their experience working on teams include:

1. Do you prefer to work as part of a team or independently?
2. How has teamwork helped you accomplish something you could never have achieved yourself?
3. What actions and support, in your experience, make a nursing team function successfully?

4. Have you been on a nursing team that struggled or failed to work effectively together? What do you assess as the reasons for the failure?
5. What do you do consistently in your practice to provide team backup to other team members?
6. Have you ever sacrificed your agenda for the success of the team?
7. What role do you usually play when you're in a team situation?
8. How would your former team members describe your work?
9. Regarding group dynamics, what do you think hinders team-work the most?
10. How do you manage conflicts with other team members?

READ AND LISTEN TO LEAD TEAMS – FREE RESOURCES

Agency for Healthcare Quality and Research (AHRQ): TeamSTEPPS is an evidence-based set of teamwork tools to optimize patient outcomes by improving communication and teamwork skills among healthcare professionals. Most of the materials on this website are free and down-loadable for use in your organization. https://www.ahrq.gov/teamstepps/index.html

Coaching for Leaders Podcast: This excellent weekly podcast by Dave Stachowiak is designed to provide practice wisdom about team leadership. Dave (a former Dale Carnegie executive leader) runs a global leadership academy and has interviewed leading experts on the podcast since 2011. You can subscribe for free at Coaching for Leaders - Leadership podcast by Dave Stachowiak

Emerging RN Leader Website: Author Dr. Rose O Sherman posts twice weekly blogs (Monday and Thursday) on leadership topics to develop healthcare teams and nursing leaders. Many blogs include free leadership resources. https://www.emergingrnleader.com

Gallup on Teamwork: A website with many resources to improve teamwork and collaboration. https://www.gallup.com/cliftonstrengths/en/278225/how-to-improve-teamwork.aspx

Google ReWork Project Aristotle: Google has made available for free the tools they use at Google with their teams. Guides, assessments, and other tools can be downloaded and customized for your organization. https://rework.withgoogle.com/guides/

Teamwork – A Better Way: A very insightful weekly podcast where Hosts Spencer Horn and Christian Napier discuss a better way to build and strengthen teams in any organization. You can subscribe for free at https://podcasts.apple.com/us/podcast/teamwork-a-better-way/id1503812785

TedTalks on Teamwork: Amy Edmondson – How to Turn a Group of Strangers into a Team – more than 3 million views. Business school professor Amy Edmondson studies "teaming," where people come together quickly (often temporarily) to solve new, urgent, or unusual problems. Edmondson shares the elements needed to turn a group of strangers into a quick-thinking team that can nimbly respond to challenges.

The Teamwork Advantage: An excellent weekly podcast by Gregg Gregory, who conducts informal and insightful conversations with professionals and experts in the TLC arena - Teamwork, Leadership, and Culture. You can subscribe for free at https://podcasts.apple.com/us/podcast/the-teamwork-advantage-a-gregg-gregory-podcast/id1515800744

About the Author

Rose O. Sherman, EdD, RN, NEA-BC, FAAN, is nationally known for helping current and future nurse leaders to develop their leadership skills. Rose is an emeritus professor at Florida Atlantic University and is a faculty member in the Marian K Shaughnessy Nursing Leadership Academy at Case Western Reserve University. Rose received a BA in Political Science and BSN in Nursing from the University of Florida. Her master's degree in nursing is from the Catholic University of America, and her doctorate in nursing leadership is from Columbia University in New York City. Before teaching, she spent 25 years in leadership roles with the Department of Veterans Affairs at five VA Medical Centers. Rose is the Editor of *Nurse Leader,* the American Organization of Nurse Executives' official journal. She writes a popular leadership blog, www.emergingrnleader.com, read by thousands of nurse leaders weekly. Rose is a Fellow of the American Academy of Nursing and an alumnus of the Robert Wood Johnson Executive Nurse Fellowship program. She is a Gallup-certified strengths coach and author of the books, *The Nurse Leader Coach: Become the Boss No One Wants to Leave* and *The Nuts and Bolts of Nursing Leadership: Your Toolkit for Success.* In 2020, Rose received the Pioneering Spirit Award from the American Association of Critical Care nurses for her innovative work in developing nurse leaders. Contact Rose at roseosherman@outlook.com

BRING A WORKSHOP TO YOUR ORGANIZATION

Serving as a nurse leader in today's environment is challenging. From rebuilding teams to nurse leader coaching to the nuts and bolts of leadership, let us design a customized, affordable workshop to give your team the essential skills they need. Before developing the program, we will assess your needs to plan content tailored to your organization. Our highly interactive workshops are delivered onsite, virtually, or using a hybrid approach. We design our programs to give your team actionable strategies they can use immediately and the confidence they need to succeed in their role. You can learn more by contacting Rose O. Sherman at roseosherman@outlook.com

START A LEADERSHIP BOOK CLUB

This book can help catalyze a leadership team discussion about nursing care delivery redesign. Your talented nurses usually provide the best solutions to health system challenges. You can download a free book club guide at https://emergingrnleader.com/the-nurse-leader-coach/